Natural Dog

BY LISA S. NEWMAN, N.D., Ph.D

Foreword by Deborah C. Mallu, D.V.M., C.V.A.

THE CROSSING PRESS
FREEDOM, CALIFORNIA

For information on bulk purchases or group discounts for this and other
Crossing Press titles, please contact our Special Sales Manager at
800/777-1048. Visit our web site: **www.crossingpress.com**

Cautionary Note: The nutritional information, recipes, and instructions contained within this book are in no way intended as a substitute
for medical counseling. Please do not attempt self-treatment of a medical problem without consulting a qualified health practitioner.

The author and The Crossing Press expressly disclaim any and all lia-
bility for any claims, damages, losses, judgments, expenses, costs, and
liabilities of any kind or injuries resulting from any products offered
in this book by participating companies and their employees or agents.
Nor does the inclusion of any resource group or company listed within this book constitute an endorsement or guarantee of quality by the
author or The Crossing Press.

Library of Congress Cataloging-in-Publication Data

Newman, Lisa S.
    Natural dog / by Lisa S. Newman.
        p. cm. -- (The Crossing Press pocket series)
    At head of title: Natural pet care.
    ISBN 1-58091-000-9 (pbk.)
    1. Dogs 2. Dogs--Health. 3. Dogs--Diseases--Alternative
treatment. 4. Holistic veterinary medicine. I. Title. II. Title:
Natural pet care. III. Series.
SF427.N48   1999
636.7'0893--dc21   99-37371
                                                              CIP

Contents

Foreword

It is with great pleasure that I introduce Lisa Newman's remarkable series. She has dedicated her life to helping you care for your animal companions—we can all benefit from her years of experience.

We are living in a time of great change, especially in the realm of health care. As a practicing veterinarian for more than two decades, I have witnessed both myself and my clients begin to seek less invasive, more natural methods for healing our dogs and cats. Once we understood that all beings are interconnected on this planet, we became aware that our thoughts, emotions, and family dynamics played an important role in the health of our animal companions. We began to realize the importance of forming a team first with the members of our animal family, aided by other healing professionals including natural health counselors and animal communicators.

Over the years I have heard people say, "I didn't know you could use that natural remedy or treatment on animals." Feel confident that you can help your animal companions where the healing is best—in your loving home. Our animals nurture us by giving us unconditional love. In turn, we can nurture them with fresh, live food and supplements, so that they can live a long and healthy life. Lisa Newman will show you the way so that you can be empowered as a healer.

Deborah C. Mallu, D.V.M., C.V.A.

The Natural Dog

Today's dog breeds are the result of intense domestication and increasing genetic manipulation, resulting in many dogs struggling with physical or behavioral issues. Certain breeds have become popular at different times: the elegant French Poodle during the twenties and thirties, the Boxer in the forties, the Doberman Pinscher in the seventies. Other breeds also have become popular because of the movies—from *Lassie*, the loyal Collie, to *101 Dalmatians*. Such specialization has changed the genetic codes in favor of appearance, size, and color, but has also mutated the genetic information for health and emotional stability. As a result, many pet owners are presently faced with problems we have not seen before in dog health or behavior.

Inbreeding and excessive genetic manipulation has minimized our animals' natural ability to cure themselves. Moreover, years of vaccinations, chemical baths, flea/tick potions, dips or sprays, medications, and most importantly, poor-quality ingredients, artificial colors, preservatives, and by-products found in most pet foods and treats eventually take their toll.

Cancer is one of the most dreaded diseases today, along with premature aging. Both conditions often have been preceded by a long history of neglected or suppressed symptoms. Whether these symptoms are considered isolated—or the result of a specific disease or organ failure—over ninety-five percent of these symptoms are preventable with proper care. Behavioral issues are also on the rise, as more dogs exhibit aggressive or fearful attitudes and have trouble learning to get along with their human families. Although many breeds are predisposed towards these behaviors, they are more likely to be triggered by chemicals and sugar in their diet, and by early experiences of abandonment or mistreatment. It is obvious then, that these behaviors are preventable, regardless of "poor" genetics. This is what holistic animal care is all about: to help you support the most positive genetic potential your pet has, and thus to prevent or reverse problems.

UNDERSTANDING YOUR DOG'S BEHAVIOR

Dogs are pack animals who crave the familiar provided by close family contact. Love is as vital to them as the air they breathe. If they cannot be near you and be allowed to live within the family unit, they will seek contact any way they can, including drawing negative attention to themselves.

Dogs who are left outside or kenneled for the major part of the day live shorter lives and suffer a higher incidence of behavioral or physical problems. Even if you are away at work, if they have access to both the house and the yard, they will feel they are contributing by protecting the family "cave." If you leave them isolated in one area of the house or outside, they will feel that they have been banished from the family cave. The resulting stress will affect them, and, whether you notice it or not, will eventually manifest itself as a symptom evident in the dog's behavior and in its body.

The basic problem is one of miscommunication—you and your dog are speaking two different languages. Imagine for a moment that you are in a foreign land trying to understand your tour guide, who doesn't speak English. What a relief it is when you work out some familiar signals. Dogs are looking at us constantly for such signals, trying to decipher what we are saying, because they desperately want to please us. Begin understanding your dog by putting yourself in his or her paws.

Ask yourself if your dog can rely on:

- **Your love**—consistent, fair, and gentle; focused and sincere
- **Your attention**—daily regard as to their emotional and physical well-being
- **Your care**—responsive to disorder, accident, or illness (acute or long-term)
- **Your home**—a safe and loving shelter, free of fear or stress
- **Your devotion**—through the easy, fun times *and* the difficult ones

Exploring and changing certain things to fit your dog's needs rather than your own, and regarding their well-being and raising them well can prevent a lot of struggle on both your parts.

CHOOSING THE RIGHT DOG

If you are contemplating a new addition to your family, consider what kind of dog will suit your needs, as well as your dog's needs. For example: A Terrier is bred to dig. If you are a gardener and don't like a dog digging up your flower bed, think again. A Sheltie may be small, but requires a lot of exercise, or they can become destructive. A Great Dane does not require a lot of exercise, but can be a handful for a senior citizen to train. Poodles do not shed, but do require a lot of grooming. Research the many books available to learn about the feeding, exercise, and care required of any particular breed that interests you, before you bring home a life-long partner.

TRAINING WITHOUT TRAUMA

You should never raise your hand to a puppy or grown dog—they will only think that you are attacking them. Most people hit their dog out of frustration due to poor communication. Dogs learn by repetition. It takes approximately seventy-five repetitions, hearing the command and correctly associating the desired behavior with that command, before you can rely on the fact that your dog understands and is not simply reacting to you.

Be absolutely clear and consistent in the signals you are giving your dog:

- Do not say "get away" one time and "no" the next—use "No!" only as NO! and mean it.

- Do not use "NO" indiscriminately—your dog will simply become deaf to it.

- Give a warning, "NO!" If behavior continues, say it in a lower voice with more growl-tones.

- As a second warning, grab their collar or loose jowl skin and jerk it slightly.

- As a third and final warning, grab their jowl skin and pin them into submission for ten seconds (count it off).

- If the behavior escalates, isolate the dog in a quiet place no more than fifteen minutes, or they will forget the reason for the punishment. Then allow them back into the fold without fanfare.

This method of discipline closely resembles the way a bitch will discipline her pups—the way a pup is "wired." (It's their language.) Therefore, a dog will quickly respond and understand that what they did was not acceptable behavior. There is no need to chase a dog about, screaming and hitting them, or ignoring them until the problem gets worse—possibly to the point of no return.

To help your dog understand and develop a fondness for learning from you:

- Do not work with your dog when you are in a bad mood or are short-tempered.
- Begin each session with play or exercise, which will focus your dog and let off steam.
- Always use the same signals and commands—follow the same routine.
- Set aside time each day to practice communicating together by working together.
- Understand for yourself *first* what you will *teach*—*then* teach it.
- Go over a new command until the dog learns it perfectly. Do this before you begin teaching your dog a new command. This builds confidence in you and in your dog. Confusion will quickly erode effective communication.
- Always end training sessions with a few minutes of exercise/play/fun.
- End the session with your dog eager to continue learning, not freaked out.

Taking the time to train your dog properly will provide you with a better, more reliable companion. A trained dog is less likely to be destructive, to run off and get hit by a car, to hurt another pet or human, or to develop bad habits—because you are connecting with the dog and correcting such bad habits. And, due to the fact that your dog is pleasant and fun to be around, you will be spending more time with her. Consequently, your trained dog is less likely to get sick.

NOAH'S THEORY

I have long advocated that dogs should be raised in twos since they are such pack animals, and we as pack leader and primary friend are often not available to them. A doggie pal can keep another dog from going crazy and acting out, or becoming ill from turning the loneliness inward. If you have more than two dogs, you run the risk of not having enough of yourself to go around. I say—never have more dogs than you can pet yourself—at the same time! I should mention that getting another dog as a companion for your dog cannot substitute for your love and attention. You will have to care for both, and the more time and attention you take in understanding the two dogs, the greater the payoff—you will have two well-behaved dogs, rather than one neurotic one.

There is, of course, a downside of having more than one dog. If you can't afford to feed and care for two, or if you don't have the time to care for two, don't get a second dog—you will hurt both yourself and your dogs. If you can afford the time, money, and energy, but if you do not have a lot of time for your dog during the week—please consider getting another, so they can have each other's company.

The more time and attention that you take in understanding your dog and his or her needs, the easier it will be to prevent behavioral issues from ruining your relationship. A happy, well-adjusted dog is also one who is less likely to suffer from disease. Emotional stress can have as much to do with immune dysfunction and the manifestation of symptoms as diet can. A dog who is fed the very best diet and is nutritionally supplemented, but lives stressed-out or fearful all the time—will have trouble assimilating nutrients and maintaining good health. Providing a loving, stable home will help support your dog's well-being as much as anything else you can do.

Holistic Animal Care

Holistic animal care addresses the entire body rather than its parts, encompassing the body, mind, spirit, and even the environment. The application of various modalities is done in a synergistic way to help stimulate, strengthen, and support the body's own biological processes and natural defenses. This care is used as a means of preventing as well as reversing biological imbalances which can lead to health or behavioral problems.

Nutrition is central to holistic animal care. It can often be the deciding factor between emotional wellness, health, and disease. Poor nutrition will quickly lead to an imbalance, cripple the body's curative abilities, and possibly create behavioral problems. Regardless of the amount of attention, drugs, or natural remedies given to dogs, if they are not receiving adequate nutrition, their own curative response is hindered.

Nutrition is also the cornerstone of a modality known as naturopathy. Defined by a medical dictionary as a "drugless system of therapy by the use of physical forces, such as air, light, water, heat, massage, etc.," naturopathy emphasizes supporting the body's physical attempts to eliminate disease. Naturopaths believe that a major cause of disease is an excessive build-up of toxic materials (often due to improper eating and lack of exercise) which clog the eliminatory system. Various techniques are used to detoxify and stimulate the body, so that symptoms and disease are reversed. Dogs are put on supportive programs of high-quality nutrition, proper food-combining (to stimulate and aid digestion), and the judicious use of nutritional supplements and herbs. Prevention is considered the best cure.

Basic to folk medicine and every culture since ancient times, herbs are probably the oldest known remedies used to stimulate healing. It is widely believed that people began using herbs after observing how animals in the wild would instinctively select appropriate herbs when they were ill. In herbology, leaves, roots, bark, flowers, and seeds are used to assist the healing process primarily by helping the body to eliminate and to detoxify. Herbs provide a slower and deeper action than prescription drugs. They are quickly becoming mainstream, with a growing presence in regular drugstores and supermarket chains.

Another modality, which provides an even slower and deeper action, is homeopathy. Sometimes nutrition or herbs won't be enough—they may begin the cleansing process and support the body (by strengthening it so that it can go through the necessary curative process), but often it is the homeopathic remedy that will stimulate a deeper level of healing. The real beauty of the homeopathic system lies in the simplicity of its basic principles and in the safety of its remedies, which have been exhaustively researched and used successfully for hundreds of years.

The German physician, Samuel Hahnemann, founded homeopathy based on one basic principle that has held true ever since homeopathy was originated in the late 1700s: that like is cured by like—that a substance that can mimic symptoms can cure them as well. This principle revolutionized the understanding of symptoms and disease.

Hahnemann noted certain similarities between symptoms produced by some diseases and by the drugs used to treat them. From this he established his "Law of Similars," which identified the principle that a disease could be cured by whatever medicine produced similar symptoms when given to a healthy person. The point of homeopathy is that the treatment works with, rather than against, the body's own efforts to regain health.

Bee venom is an example of how homeopathy works. We know that a bee sting causes a topical reaction, including swelling, fluid accumulation, redness of the skin, pain, and soreness, a reaction that is accentuated by heat or pressure. Some sensitive animals will also experience such behavioral symptoms as apathy, stupor, listlessness, or the opposite, whining or fear. When a homeopathically prepared dilute solution of the venom (known as Apis) is given to a pet with these symptoms—even if they are caused by something other than a bee sting—the condition will soon begin to clear up. The essential key is that the symptoms are quite similar to what the remedy, in its undiluted state, would create.

Flower essences (which balance emotional states) and tissue cells salts (which support physiological processes) act similarly, by stimulating the body's own natural healing and re-establishing homeostasis.

THE HOLISTIC PET

I define a holistically reared pet to be in a state of balance on three interrelated levels: the physical, the emotional, and the environmental. A healthy pet has vitality and is free from physiological malfunction, possesses emotional clarity resulting in good behavior and happiness, and receives (as well as contributes) joy, love, and security in their living environment.

This is the opposite of a chemically reared dog, who is often in a state of imbalance or dis-ease. This dog suffers from chronic symptoms and lacks vitality. Such a dog is generally unbalanced, with a body that is constantly assaulted by substances that a healthy dog would have no problem processing: allergens, viruses, bacteria, toxins, worms.

Every person who owns a dog should in truth be a caregiver, helping its natural curative process—rather than merely suppressing the dog's symptoms, which are simply evidence of its imbalance. The premise of holistic animal care is this: Treat the body well and the body will be well. By providing your pet with ample love, quality nutrition, proper supplementation, and holistic modalities when appropriate, your dog will remain balanced. If the dog is then assaulted by certain substances, its innate ability to cure itself will kick in, restoring balance.

UNDERSTANDING THE UNHEALTHY DOG

Most dogs who are chronically ill are suffering the consequences of long-term exposure to an emotionally and/or physically toxic environment as well to its ingestion of chemicals. Chemicals alter the primary biological functions in the body, place undue stress on the vital organs and glands, and destroy healthy tissue. The result is a body out of balance or dis-eased.

Most dogs that are not healthy have been exposed to:

- Standard commercial pet foods and artificially made treats that are sweetened or yeast-based
- Shotgun medications (the indiscriminate use of standard medications)
- Excessive vaccinations and yearly boosters—especially during surgical procedures
- Toxic cleaning products and pest control products (especially collars or monthly drug doses)

- Environmental pollution (without the benefit of regular detoxification)
- An emotionally and/or physically stressful living environment (past and present)

I believe that commercial pet food and treats account for the largest assault on dogs' bodies and are the primary reason pets develop symptoms. I am not talking about food allergies here. It is my belief that the quality (or lack of good fresh quality) of the ingredient can do more harm than the ingredient itself. Many dogs that previously tested positive for an allergy to a certain food are now eating it without any problems. The answer is simple—holistic animal care has reversed the symptoms and the so-called allergy. The by-products and meat, certified as unfit for human consumption, present in most commercial pet foods severely compromise the dog's ability to digest and assimilate nutrients. The artificial colors or flavors, chemical preservatives, nitrates, and rancid animal fats present in commercial pet food similarly interfere with digestion. Poorly digested matter becomes harder to eliminate, causing a back-up of old fecal material in the bowel, which further prohibits assimilation of vital nutrients.

Pets often aren't given the opportunity to run and can't always go outside to move their bowels. A dog fed poor food loaded with chemicals and by-products will not be able to properly digest the food. This undigested matter moves into the colon, but since complete evacuation is not really possible, the fecal matter will line the sides of the colon. Chemicals (such as ethoxyquin, a commonly used pet food preservative that is a moisture prohibitive) limit the lubrication necessary for a properly evacuated stool, and the fecal material hardens, finally producing small, hard, dry stools that the dog is able to pass.

Many companies state that their pet food is "more digestible with less waste," but what do you think a physician would say to you if you described your own stools as small, hard lumps? Certainly, a better-quality food will produce less stool volume (generally due to less fillers and better digestibility), but it should not be caused by the lack of moisture in the stool. The colon requires ample hydration to function properly. Always provide fresh, filtered drinking water.

As old fecal material builds up inside the colon, it becomes harder and harder for the body to clean out this material on its own. This interferes with the body's ability to absorb or "ventilate" nutrients from digested matter in the colon into the bloodstream for distribution among the body's hungry cells and energy-depleted organ systems.

The harder the ingredients are to break down and process and the more chemicals that are present, the more stress is placed on the body. The harder the body has to work, the quicker it breaks down and falls apart. Due to improper digestion and assimilation, the body lacks the resources to utilize whatever nutrients that are entering. These nutrients are vital to proper biological processes such as the immune system. Improper digestion and assimilation also lead to a build-up of general waste (toxins) in the body, placing a huge burden upon the eliminatory organs. As the liver and kidneys become overburdened, the body attempts to detoxify through the largest eliminatory organ it has, the skin. Hence, skin and coat problems emerge. These are most commonly diagnosed as allergies. Additionally, the lymph system and endocrine system are over-stimulated, possibly leading to the development of a deeper, more serious disease, such as reactive arthritis or cancer.

The next most common cause of dogs' ill health is their exposure to chemicals and irritants in other, non-dietary, forms. This can be as simple as a chemical-based breath mint given as a treat, or as complicated as annual vaccination boosters. Included in this list of irritants are artificially perfumed shampoos, medicated skin treatments, flea or tick control products, household cleaning agents, and long-term medication. If you think of the body as a healthy balanced scale, and you keep adding chemicals to one side, the scale will be tipped off-balance. But if you keep good nutrition replenished on one side and minimize the build-up of chemicals on the other, this scale stays in balance, and the body stays healthy.

There are other factors that may cause a state of imbalance. Structural imbalances are often a prime underlying cause of dis-ease. Old injuries or genetic malfunctions such as rheumatoid arthritis, can place stress on certain organ systems. A build-up of calcium deposits and joint or spinal inflammation may also put pressure on the specific nerves involved with digestive organs, such as the stomach. This can interfere with normal stomach functioning, leading to improper digestion and poor assimilation of nutrients. Often, addressing the structural problems will help reverse the chronic condition. Chiropractic adjustments, massage, acupressure, and acupuncture can help you reverse your dog's symptoms.

There are other causes of a dog's imbalance. Negative emotions and environment are often overlooked. Have you ever felt butterflies in your stomach and had diarrhea due to a stressful situation? Pets who frequently experience extreme emotions (fear, nervousness, and tension) are also more likely to suffer from behavioral issues, digestive problems, and glandular imbalance. Dogs experience stress due to family changes such as relocating, members leaving or dying, divorce, new births, new jobs, etc.

The pituitary, adrenal, and thyroid glands are very susceptible to hyperstimulation and exhaustion brought on by chronic emotional stress. These glands are associated with the fight-or-flight reaction to negative stimulus that is common to all living beings. Therefore, it is important to provide a safe and nurturing environment for your pet. Nutritional supplementation and remedies (especially flower essences) that re-balance the emotions are very helpful—they often can be the key to a more complete physical healing.

When an animal's health is out of balance, waste builds up in the bloodstream and burdens the eliminatory organs. Urea, the normal waste product of meat protein metabolism, is often the culprit, accounting for the large number of pets who test positive for meat allergies. The poorer the quality of meat and the more difficult it is to digest, the more waste products are produced during its digestion. As urea builds up in the body, a gout-like reaction may occur. Because it is difficult to break down, yeast can burden the liver. However, the trouble is that yeast is found in practically all commercial pet foods.

Urea or yeast toxicity manifests itself in certain symptoms, most notably:

- Known or suspected allergies to yeast, beef, pork, meat, meat by-products, or meal
- Ear infections, eye discharges, and upper respiratory problems, including asthma
- Excessive licking and chewing of paws, resulting in lick granuloma

- Prickly heat-type rashes, itchy skin, with or without hot spots, pimples, or pustules
- Slower healing of skin problems
- Excessive loss of hair or coat condition
- Foul-smelling breath, flatulence, and/or stool (especially with mucus or off-colored)
- Increased fatty tumor, cyst, or cancerous tumor production
- Poor digestion and assimilation of nutrients
- Blood sugar instability, diabetes
- High levels of liver enzymes and eosinophils detected (represents a damaged liver)
- Decreased phosphates found in the urine (due to kidney disease)
- Liver, pancreatic, gall bladder, and kidney dysfunction or failure
- Weakened immune responses, especially chronic infections or cancer
- Premature aging, with or without chronic arthritic or digestive symptoms
- Neurological issues, including seizures
- Aggression and other training or behavioral problems
- Increased sensitivities to pollution, vaccinations, and chemicals in general
- Parasitic infestation, especially fleas and ticks (which feed off of skin-eliminated waste)

I have since seen research which indicates that using garlic by itself is more powerful against flea and tick infestations than yeast used alone or yeast in combination with garlic. A clean diet, which results in fewer waste products, greatly reduces the waste that must be eliminated through the skin. Excess waste is the very thing that attracts a flea or tick to the body in the first place and then feeds them. Old fecal material in the colon also attracts and feeds internal parasites such as worms.

As urea, metabolized yeast, and other excessive wastes build up in the body and undue stress is placed upon vital organs, it is not uncommon for the body to begin experiencing system malfunctions. This vicious cycle is clearly identifiable if you know what to look for. First, the digestive system is affected, making it even harder to break down ingredients. More waste products are circulating, and less nutrients are available. Then the eliminatory system becomes burdened, placing undue stress upon the lymphatic and immune systems. Chronic symptoms develop, which usually are suppressed with medication. Once medication is stopped, the symptoms return and the cycle continues. Ultimately, there is organ and gland malfunction, possibly leading to early death. Frequently, the illness may seem to come out of nowhere. You might exclaim, "Yesterday he was so healthy," but this kind of breakdown does not happen overnight. It takes time for the body to become so overburdened, and there are always early warning signs that this breakdown is taking place.

Any pet suffering from poor health related to genetics, sensitivities, allergies, or toxicity can truly benefit from holistic animal care. A wholesome, toxin-free approach to diet and environment can not only prevent a symptom, it can help reverse it more quickly and effectively than the further application of chemicals.

When pets with chronic dis-eases are placed on an ongoing holistic animal care lifestyle program, the results can be miraculous. As each month passes and the body gets stronger, it becomes less and less sensitive to toxins. The animal then exhibits less severe symptoms with each cycle, becoming easier to treat each time. Current acute symptoms are reversed more quickly. Dogs who are healthy to begin with will realize their full genetic potential. You won't know this until you see the results and can compare your dog before and after holistic animal care.

Once a better diet is implemented, don't stop detoxification and supplementation immediately after the symptoms have been suppressed. If you do so, the body will become burdened again (having already shown a predisposition to this weakness) and will again react to allergens or stress. Continue supporting the immune system with a correct diet in order to prevent reoccurrence of such symptoms.

Treating your pet's symptoms holistically is the quickest, most effective way to completely reverse an underlying condition. In those animals that have been genetically or environmentally predisposed to deeper disease, holistic animal care will, in the long run, serve to minimize degenerative possibilities and maximize what curative potential there is.

Nutrition...
as Nature Intended!

The primary line of defense in preventing or treating symptoms is a sound nutritional program. Your pet's natural diet should consist of fresh, high-quality ingredients that are easy to digest and assimilate. Home cooking is optimal, but might not be practical for you. Therefore, you must be very careful to seek out a quality commercial product. Become an educated label reader. Look beyond catchy terms such as "natural," "organic," "healthy," "symptom-related diet," and "human-grade quality." Ask the manufacturer directly to prove their quality and guarantee their formula.

Seek out only Grade A or B meats (human grade). Avoid the four-D meats: dead, dying, diseased, or disabled animals not fit for human consumption. Four-D meats are commonly used in pet foods. Grain by-products also present a big problem in commercial pet products. Wheat millings, brewer's rice (leftovers from brewing), and flours are inexpensive fillers devoid of nutritional value, that can severely compromise your dog's health. Often these grains are purchased rancid and moldy (to save money), adding to the possibility of a toxic reaction. Grade 1 or 2 grains (all human grades) should be used, preferably whole ground, to ensure that their nutritional goodness remains intact. Go for the best quality you can afford—think of it as an insurance policy against poor health and future expenses.

Beware of "lite" diets—they may actually cause weight gain in the long run. Filler may be filling, but it is devoid of nutrients. The brain decides if there is enough nutrition available, regardless of the diet, and stores calories to ward off starvation. A properly balanced, quality diet that provides easy to assimilate nutrients will naturally bring your dog to the proper weight.

People are often concerned that changing their dog's diet will only result in digestive upsets. This is true, if you are changing from one poor-quality or chemical-based diet to another! When switching to a healthier, more natural diet, there should be no irritating ingredients to upset the balance. Often, the biggest problem during the transition may be soft stool and gas, due to the fact that you probably are overfeeding your dog on the new diet.

One cup of a grocery store food is full of filler, almost fifty percent worth. When you shift to a higher-quality food, there is generally less filler involved. Therefore, feeding the same quantities (cup for cup) will result in overfeeding and gastric upset. Your best bet is to read and follow the manufacturer's specific recommendations for the new food, and then watch your pet carefully for the first few weeks to see how it reacts.

Overfeeding often occurs when people begin cooking for their pets. I suggest that you seek out a well-researched book on natural pet care that includes homecooked recipes.

I recommend that you don't feed your dog raw meat. Although this is now becoming common, I have encountered many sick animals who have been fed such a diet. I believe that animals evolve to fit their environment, and since our pets have been domesticated for so long, they have evolved into processed food eaters. They have lost the ability to digest raw meat tissue, bone, hide, feathers, etc., on a regular basis.

Even with the use of digestive enzymes, I still see most pets struggling to digest raw animal tissue. Don't get me wrong—I prefer homecooked foods to commercially processed pet foods. The simple fact of the matter is that lightly cooking (which does not destroy enzymes and nutrients) helps to break down meat so that it is easier to digest. Frequently, meat has not been properly handled and can pass e. coli bacteria or parasites to the dog, leading to gastrointestinal distress.

I should emphasize that, even with the best-quality, balanced diet (using cooked or raw meats), nutritional supplementation is necessary to provide many nutrients now missing from our food chain. For instance, research indicates that fifty years ago spinach had up to eighty percent more nutritional value than today! This is true (in varying degrees) for other vegetables, grains, and fruits, as well as meats from animals fed off the land. Our earth has been stripped of many naturally occurring micronutrients, which used to be found in soil, and our vegetables are only as good as the dirt they grow in. Years of overfarming, the use of toxic chemicals or fertilizers, and environmental pollution such as acid rain have taken their toll.

Even organic farming cannot guarantee that the produce will be more nutritious, as it will take approximately seventy-five years before the nutrients return to the soil. Therefore, it is important that we supplement our animals' (and our own) diets to ensure that we receive the fundamental nutrients required. Even pet foods which are "nutritionally complete" according to AAFCO (American Association of Feed Control Officers) guidelines aren't complete according to what is truly needed for basic good health. For instance, the guidelines allow so much protein per cup of food, but that protein does not have to be *digestible*; therefore, it cannot be assimilated as protein! The same holds true for certain sources of Vitamin A or calcium, just to name a few. Therefore, proper nutrition not only includes quality, easy to digest foods, but also the appropriate supplementation to support optimum wellness, while stimulating your dog's curative potential.

These are the key ingredients for a healthy diet:

- Fresh ingredients with no unpleasant odor (indicating rancidity)

- Whole foods such as whole-ground grains, not "flours," "mill runs," or "by-products"

- Concentrated protein sources known as "meal" (as in "lamb meal" or "beef meal") are preferred over whole meats (listed only as "lamb"). This is not to be confused with "by-product meal" (see list of ingredients to avoid).

The term "meal" simply refers to the process of removing up to eighty percent, but no less than forty-five percent, of the ingredients' natural water content, so there is more meat protein for your money (since water only adds to the ingredients' weight). The ingredients are listed on the label by weight with the heaviest ingredient first. For instance, it is deceiving to find chicken listed first when the majority of the protein in the pet food is in reality coming from grains, not animal protein. This formula greatly reduces the cost of ingredients for the manufacturer, due to the actual amount of animal protein used.

Because one pound of meal is equal to approximately three pounds of whole meat, and there is an additional charge to dehydrate the meat, meal is expensive to produce. Therefore, many companies use the meat to draw you to the label, but use a cheaper ingredient for the actual protein—one that may trigger allergies. This is true for all chicken, turkey, rabbit, fish, and other animal protein sources used in commercial pet foods.

Look for the following ingredients on your pet food label:

- Identifiable, digestible animal protein or fat sources such as beef, beef meal, lamb, lamb meal, lamb fat, chicken, chicken meal or chicken fats, turkey, ostrich, etc., not vague terms like "meats," "mammal," or "animal fats"

- USDA Grade A or B animal protein sources, preferably raised without growth hormones or recently given antibiotics

- USDA Grade 1 or 2 whole grains, preferably free of chemical pesticides or herbicides. Organic grains are not cost-effective in commercial pet foods. If the label on the food you are feeding your pet says "organic," demand written certification, and check that it is not organic by-products. However, "pesticide-free" is available, or "washed" grains are possible. For home-cooking, go for the best ingredients you can afford!

- Balanced, combined ingredients of proteins and grain sources seems to suit most pets better than a single ingredient, contrary to popular belief.

- Vegetable and fruit fiber should be present (for example, carrots and apples) for proper digestion, natural flavoring, and trace nutrients. Fiber in general is very important to proper elimination. Moreover, fiber (additionally provided in whole grains) is full of vital nutrients.

- Quality sources of fat (necessary for energy and good coats) such as vegetable or fish oils should be used, rather than animal fats. This holds true even for high-energy dogs.

- Remember that you generally get what you pay for! If you pay $10.00 for a 40-pound bag of food, and the cost of making and marketing the product is as follows: paper bag 85 cents, shipping $1.00, advertising and handling 75 cents, yielding a $2.50 profit for the manufacturer, $1.25 for the wholesaler, and $2.25 for the retailer—how much do you think the manufacturer actually spent on the ingredients?

- Take into consideration how much of the cheaper food you will need to sustain your pet. Often, the cheaper foods will prove to be more expensive, due to the fact that you have to use so much more food than you would with a better-quality diet, which contains less filler.

- Product should be fresh when purchased. If you bought fresh-baked bread, it would still be wonderful to eat the next day, but would you still be eating it two weeks later? Be sure to check the date the food was packed. Never use food (especially naturally preserved diets) that is older than six months, unless it is packaged in a completely sealed, airtight, barrier bag. Stale food has not only lost its flavor, but also most of its nutritional value through oxidation.

These are ingredients to avoid in a healthy diet:

- Chemical preservatives: Ethoxyquin, BHA and/or BHT, Propylene Glycol, Nitrates
- Artificial flavors or colors
- Foul-smelling ingredients must be avoided. If the food smells like traditional pet food (you know that smell, even in fresh bags it smells rancid) throw it out.
- Greasy food, that leaves smelly oil on the bag or a sheen on canned formulas, indicates that it is heavy in animal fats or tallow (rendered carcasses and recycled cooking grease from restaurants). These are difficult to digest and are most often rancid prior to manufacturing. This accounts for that rancid "dog food" smell, even in "fresh" bags.
- Animal by-products such as "beef by-product," "lamb by-product," "chicken by-product" (a mixture of the *whole carcass* including feces, cancerous tumors, hide, hooves, beaks, feathers, and fur). Also avoid their mysterious cousins: "meat" or "meat

by-products" (a mixture of whatever mammals, including road kill, rats, and other dogs and cats that got ground up together), "fish by-products," and "poultry by-products" (a mixture of whatever feathered animals got ground up together, including pigeons)—Need I say more?

- Grain by-products ("mill runs," "flours," "middlings," "husks," "parts") should be avoided at all costs. Not only have they had all their nutritionally rich parts removed, they may irritate the digestive and eliminatory tracts. These grain by-products are cheap fillers used as a protein source (although they cannot be digested and therefore cannot be assimilated) to increase the finished product's weight and mass.

- Soybeans—dogs cannot digest them. Canine digestion lacks an amino acid necessary to digest soybeans. Because tofu and soybean oil are already processed they can be tolerated by many dogs. However, most pet foods contain soybeans, which can trigger bloat, an often fatal digestive reaction.

- Fillers such as powdered "cellulose," or "cellulose fiber," can include recycled newspaper, sawdust, and cardboard. "Plant cellulose" usually means ground peanut hulls, which are very damaging to sensitive colon tissues. Beet pulp or grain by-products have no nutritional value, but do add bulk and weight to the finished product.

- Yeast is a cheap source of B Vitamins, amino acids, and some nutrients. It also adds natural flavor and color. It is touted for flea control and a shiny coat, but it can contribute to symptoms by burdening the liver and interfering in proper digestion.

- Sugar is added to most commercial diets and treats. It is labeled as "sucrose," "beet pulp," "molasses," "cane syrup," "fruit solids," and, of course, "sugar." It is a very cheap, heavy filler which is addictive to dogs. Additional sugar in the diet is the primary trigger of weight problems, diabetic conditions, and behavioral problems in pets today.

I recommend supplementing the food you feed your dog (no matter how good it is) with a well-balanced vitamin and mineral supplement. Seek out a high-quality, high-potency, daily multiple. Food-source supplements are excellent choices for the general maintenance of healthy dogs, but they are not potent enough to prevent or reverse significant disease in a genetically compromised or chronically ill pet. Be sure that you provide at least the minimum requirements of vital nutrients, because, for whatever reason, your dog may not be able to assimilate its food completely. It is additional insurance. I recommend these nutrients daily for a medium-sized (fifty-pound) dog:

- Vitamin A (5,000 mg.) for a strong immune system, eyes, tissue; repairs several other biological processes
- Beta Carotene (2,500 mg.) to support Vitamin A assimilation
- Vitamin B1 (50 mg.) for energy and emotional well-being
- Vitamin B2 (50 mg.) necessary for fat and carbohydrate metabolism, especially to promote curative response
- Vitamin B6 (50 mg.) for red blood cell production and protein metabolism; primary immune nutrient
- Vitamin B12 (50 mcg.) aids in calcium absorption; is anti-inflammatory and necessary to symptom reversal
- Vitamin D (100 I.U.) with Vitamin A helps cat utilize calcium and phosphorus; essential for healthy thyroid
- Vitamin E (25 I.U.) is an exceptional antioxidant, triggers tissue repair; oxygenates the tissues
- Niacin (50 mg.) promotes healthy skin and nerves; supports digestion, metabolism, and detoxification
- Pantothenic Acid (50 mg.) is an anti-oxidant vital to adrenal activity; developing antibodies and reducing toxins

- Folic Acid (200 mcg.) necessary for DNA, enzyme efficiency, and blood; reduces malabsorption problems

- Choline (50 mg.) vital neurotransmitter; works with Inositol to emulsify fats; supports liver function

- Inositol (50 mg.) lowers fatty deposits in the liver; controls cholesterol and benefits the diabetic

- PABA (50 mg.) protects skin from sun-related cancer; supports coat color; may reduce skin tag growths

- Biotin (50 mcg.) aids metabolism of fatty acids and amino acids; makes antibodies; promotes good coat condition

- Vitamin C (125 mg.) repairs connective tissue; builds resistance to cancer, allergies, bacteria, or viruses

- Calcium (25 mg.) needed for strong bones and teeth; reduces muscular stress; inhances colon condition

- Phosphorus (10 mg.) supports structure, oxygen to the brain, maintains pH, reduces muscular fatigue

- Magnesium (3.5 mg.) critical for bones, nerve, and muscle function; works with calcium to regulate the heart

- Potassium (5 mg.) supports electrolyte and pH balance, neurotransmitter; vital for optimum cardiovascular health

- Iron (9 mg.) combines with copper and proteins to form red blood cells necessary to oxygenate the body

- Manganese (3 mg.) nourishes the brain, nerves; supports SOD and anti-oxidant activities; eliminates pain

- Zinc (8 mg.) co-enzyme of SOD—protects against free radicals which may promote cancer and other diseases

- Iodine (75 mcg.) vital to proper thyroid function and proper metabolism; tissue development and repairs

- Copper (125 mcg.) for inflammatory response, bone mineralization, coat color; necessary for protein metabolism

- Glutamic Acid (12 mg.) supports nerve health; metabolizes fats and sugars; detoxifies ammonia in the brain
- Selenium and Chromium (12 mcg.) are immune-stimulating minerals which reduce premature aging

To introduce a dietary change and to kick off a successful program for prevention or rehabilitation, begin by imposing a twenty-four hour period of fasting. Many people associate fasting with enforced starvation. This couldn't be further from the truth—fasting can save your dog's life!

Fasting encourages the body to detoxify and re-balance. The fasting methods I suggest are safe and gentle. The pleading, begging look your pet might give you at dinnertime may bother you the most. Twenty-five percent of that look may be hunger-related, but the other seventy-five percent is definitely control-related. Pets, particularly dogs, are experts at controlling their masters.

To avoid that pleading look while your dog is fasting, do something fun with her at her usual dinnertime. Bring home a new toy (but don't do it out of guilt!), or take your friend out for a fifteen-minute walk. Your dog will get the exercise, and neither you nor the dog will be thinking about food. If you still feel guilty, just remind yourself that they are *begging for their life*.

Anyone who has tried to clean a counter with a dirty sponge knows that a clean sponge is more effective. During a fast, old fecal material will be expelled from the colon while vital eliminatory organs, such as the kidneys and liver, will get a break from their job of processing daily waste, thus allowing for a deeper elimination of backed-up toxins. This results in improved digestive and eliminatory systems. Good processing is necessary for the intake of both nutrients and therapeutic substances (which will help strengthen the immune system and build resistance to sensitivities). The reduction of toxins in the body also improves the overall condition of your dog, and sometimes will help reverse most symptoms. It is common, following a short fast and detoxification, that the more obvious symptoms immediately will begin to improve. Even a short twenty-four hour fast with homeopathic support can make a world of difference.

Usually within the first six to eight weeks after detoxification, you will see a reversal of symptoms. I have observed that seventy-five percent of dogs that have been detoxed and given a better diet along with basic nutritional support, will be healthier and happier. In the remaining twenty-five percent of cases, including those with true allergies or chronic debilitating dis-ease, the judicious use of homeopathic, herbal, and nutritional supplementation in a *continuing* course of treatment will definitely strengthen each animal's constitution and reduce or eventually eliminate their condition. With chronic cases, it can often take several weeks, even a year, to build up the body enough to eliminate the symptoms completely.

Simply suppressing symptoms pharmaceutically is not only frustrating, but may lead to a premature death. Year after year toxins attacking a body—barely protected by a struggling immune system—will only serve to weaken the body further. A sound nutritional program supported with ongoing detoxification, proper supplementation, and rebalancing with homeopathic remedies or herbs, while avoiding (or at least limiting) vaccination boosters, chemicals, and drugs, is the best way to strengthen your dog's immune system and thereby lead to his health and happiness.

The first step to take now towards establishing a successful holistic animal care program is proper detoxification.

Detoxification prepares the body to digest and assimilate nutrients that are vital to heal and strengthen your dog. No matter what wonderful new products you feed your pet, if the pet cannot properly utilize a product's nutritive or therapeutic properties, the end results will probably be disappointing. In fact, without proper detoxification, you are severely limiting the body's overall curative potential.

There are gentle and effective ways to trigger the body's eliminatory systems (the kidneys, liver, lungs, skin, and lymph system) to process waste removal on a deeper level than what is required for daily maintenance. By utilizing these methods, you will help your dog to prevent symptoms from occurring, and you will also help your dog to reverse and possibly completely eliminate disease.

Detoxification and Fasting

DETOXIFICATION THROUGH FASTING

Fasting is the method many people have used to detoxify their pets' bodies. Fasting is much more than simply withholding food. It gently rebalances the body. Be sure to always check with your veterinarian first before you start a fast, in order to be sure that there are no medical reasons that such a program is not wise at this time. Possibly you are treating your dog for diabetes and must maintain its blood sugar with food as well as insulin, or perhaps your dog is too weak to fast, due to a recent bout of minor infections. (Actually this is a perfect time to fast.)

Although I have successfully fasted many animals in such circumstances, it is always wise to rely on the advice of a trusted vet, especially if you have one who encourages you to support your dog with a holistic lifestyle.

There are two methods of detoxification that I have perfected over time and which I highly recommend.

STANDARD FAST

The standard fasting method is for pets who have acute or chronic symptoms, but who are otherwise in good health. Age makes no difference. I have seen fourteen-year-old dogs as well as sick puppies respond to this standard fast. It's pretty straightforward, assuming that your pet is fairly healthy to begin with, but you may still have to adjust the process according to your dog's specific needs.

Day One

- Feed your dog breakfast as you normally would on the morning you are to begin the fast. Simply eliminate the evening meal.
- Be sure to provide plenty of fresh drinking water.
- Provide fun-filled activity in fresh air and sunshine twice during the day, followed by a damp terry cloth rubdown.
- Be sure not to overtire or stress your pet.

Day Two—Breaking the Fast

Breaking the fast is as important as the fast itself.

- After twenty-four hours of fasting you'll feed your dog 1/2 his normal quantity of breakfast. Cooked oatmeal is a good choice for breaking the fast.
- Again provide exercise in the fresh air and sunshine twice during the day, followed by a damp terry cloth rubdown.
- Remember to give your dog plenty of water, and be sure not to overtire or stress her. If you do, you will take energy away from the curative process.
- For dinner, simply return to the normal quantity (and hopefully, better quality) of food.

To make this process really special, break the fast with *cooked oatmeal* (excellent for absorbing impurities in the digestive tract) instead of the regular diet, again at about one-half the normal quantity. A teaspoon or two of *raw honey*, encapsulated *garlic oil* (raw garlic can be too harsh at this point), and some type of *fresh green extract* such as *barley grass* or *spirulina* can be very soothing and cleansing to the digestive system after fasting. Supplements can also be added back into the diet following the fast.

This is also a good fasting protocol to follow on a weekly basis to help maintain general health and well-being. I have regularly fasted my own dogs on Mondays, and they look forward to that time. They never beg at meal time, and they don't even come to the kitchen on Monday evening. Instead, they always seem to want to chase each other just then.

You will quickly find out whether a weekly fast suits your and your dog's needs. Remember that exercise is very important at all times to help move toxins out of the body by further stimulating the eliminatory organs. The terry cloth rubdown helps to stimulate the skin (the largest eliminatory organ) and to aid it while it continues to process waste from the body's detoxification.

If an odor is present during fasting, add one-half cup baking soda to one gallon of warm, purified water, and rinse off the body, followed by drying with a towel. The baking soda will help neutralize the odor and balance the skin's pH, reducing itching. Avoid using tap water, as it contains chlorine. Chlorine is a skin irritant. If you must use tap water, boil it for fifteen minutes to evaporate the chlorine. Let the boiled tap water cool down before using. A lemon cut up and boiled in the water for twenty minutes and then strained, makes a wonderful deodorizer and acts as a disinfectant as well.

For dogs with special needs, cutting back to twenty-five to fifty percent of their standard meal, while adding supplements, herbal extracts, and vegetable and fruit juices, will increase elimination, without upsetting their metabolism.

SUPPORTIVE PHYTOCHEMICALS

Listed below are the top detoxifying herbs, vegetables, and fruits that are gentle enough to use during fasting:

• *Milk Thistle* is good for liver cleansing and support.
• *Dandelion* is a blood purifier and organ cleanser.

- *Burdock Root* helps remove catabolic waste from cellular activity.
- *Slippery Elm* is very soothing to inflamed colon tissues and helps settle the tummy.
- *Yucca*, a natural anti-inflammatory, supports circulation, and reduces discomfort.
- *Garlic*, a high-powered antibiotic is anti-bacterial, anti-viral, anti-fungal, and anti-parasitic.
- *Kombu* alkalizes the body and purifies fats from the blood.
- *Spirulina's* high chlorophyll content aids enzyme production and digestion.
- *Carrots* are trace mineral-rich and high in vitamins. They alkalize the body and are flavorful.
- *Beets* provide several supportive nutrients, fiber, and flavor.
- *Parsnips* provide wonderful support for detoxifying the kidneys.
- *Spinach* is an excellent source of nutrients and trace minerals.
- *Celery* is trace mineral-rich, and high in vitamins. It alkalizes the body promoting nutrient absorption and is flavorful.
- *Parsley* is trace mineral-rich, oxygenates the blood, helps detoxify odors and alkalizes the body.
- *Ginger* can help the digestive system, reduce gas, and aid hypertension.
- *Apples* provide needed energy while supporting detoxification.
- *Cranberries* are very high in Vitamin C and help flush urinary tract waste.
- *Papaya* balances the body, aids digestion, and flushes wastes.

Avoid harsh or highly acidic vegetables like tomatoes and onions (which can be deadly to dogs), or difficult-to-digest ingredients like cabbage. Also avoid the use of harsh fibers such as psyllium, which can further irritate and damage sensitive intestinal tissues. Although psyllium does produce bulk and encourages elimination, its negative side effects, when used alone, outweigh its benefits during detoxification.

HOMEOPATHIC DETOXIFICATION

To encourage elimination further, no matter which fasting protocol you choose, it is best to combine fasting with homeopathic detoxification. If you decide not to fast your dog or if your dog cannot be fasted for medical reasons, homeopathic detoxification works by itself and is safe for all cases. Its only drawback is that it can take almost twice as long to achieve the end result as when it is combined with fasting. On the other hand, fasting alone can take even longer to work than homeopathic remedies alone, so opt for homeopathy if you need to choose one over the other.

One or several individual homeopathic remedies may be chosen, based on your individual pet's needs. Or you may find that one of the combination products works just as well.

Homeopathy is safe to use in addition to herbs or medications, although drugs may interfere with a remedy's potential to trigger the curative process. Utilize homeopathy to its fullest potential, as it is very helpful in reducing acute flare-ups and supports symptom reversal on a deeper level than herbs or supplements alone. Although many homeopathic remedies have anti-parasitic or antibiotic actions, I recommend relying on homeopathy as a supportive, rather than sole method of eliminating parasites or infections. Homeopathy can often be the key to reversing a deeper acute or chronic weakness related to immune dysfunction.

Although a lot of emphasis is placed on potencies, I have found many remedies to be successful in a wide range of potencies, so I'm more inclined to support getting what is available to you, regardless if it is a 6X and not a 3C. For the majority of acute reactions, even if due to chronic conditions, utilizing the lower potencies will effect change. These potencies range anywhere from 3X to 30C. For long-term reversal of a specific disorder, utilizing the higher 200C potency will be effective, once the lower potencies have brought the acute reaction under control. High potencies, such as M's, should be used under professional guidance. By giving the body a boost with homeopathic remedies, other supplements act more quickly and effectively.

I recommend frequent dosing initially of a homeopathic remedy. You cannot overdose your pet. Give one dose orally, according to package instructions, every fifteen minutes for the first hour, then every hour until there is relief. To maintain relief, dose twice daily for an additional week or two. More frequent dosing can occur as needed. Resume this or any other appropriate remedy whenever the symptom presents itself and follow this schedule until there is complete reversal. Long-term maintenance is also possible through a weekly dose of the most beneficial remedy.

I prefer liquid remedies because they are easier to administer. If the dropper touches your hands or your pet, rinse it off before returning to the bottle. Most remedies come in sugar pellets (use as is) or tablets (crush inside a piece of paper first for best application). To avoid contamination and a reduction in efficacy, always allow at least fifteen minutes apart from food or strong extracts when giving homeopathic remedies, and do not handle remedies with your bare hands. Rather, use the cap or a clean piece of paper to administer the dose.

After the initial detoxification, a maintenance program can be initiated on a weekly basis. Maintenance means a single weekly dose at bedtime to help process current waste build-up, stimulate proper kidney and liver functions, and support general good health. It does not mean that homeopathic detoxification should be used in lieu of proper feeding, supplementation, and care. It simply acts as a support for functions such as digestion and elimination.

Arsenicum and *Nux Vomica* are often homeopaths' choices to establish equilibrium of biological functions and to counteract chronic symptoms. They balance the body during detoxification and counteract nausea, irritability, digestive disturbances, and liver congestion associated with detoxification. In my opinion, they should always be included in a detox program, regardless of what other remedies are chosen. The best homeopathic combinations for detoxification on the market today include these two remedies. I have reversed many acute toxic reactions (including pesticide poisonings) with *Arsenicum* and *Nux Vomica* alone. When in doubt, this is a sound combination to try.

HELPFUL HINTS TO AID GENERAL DETOXIFICATION AND THE CURATIVE PROCESS

- *Provide plenty of pure water.* Water facilitates the flushing of wastes. Avoid using tap water containing chlorine and chemicals (which may be too harsh for the kidneys), or distilled water (which may accelerate the detoxification). Your dog's drinking water should always be free of metals and sediments.
- *Groom daily* to help brush away toxins being eliminated though the skin. This also stimulates circulation, further aiding elimination and the removal of old, dead skin, and stimulating the growth of new, healthier coats. Wipe away any ear, eye, penile, vaginal, or anal discharges to avoid infections.
- *Provide daily exercise in fresh air and sunshine* to encourage circulation and respiration, which supports the removal of deeper toxins. This also improves your pet's attitude and thereby his healing.

- *Respect your dog's quiet times and needs,* even if they seem to be withdrawing from the family. It is normal for pets going through detoxification to sleep more, refuse to eat a meal or two (continuing the fasting process on their own when needed), become irritable or nervous, or to seek out warmer or cooler areas to hang out in. Do not force feed during this time, especially if fever is present.

- *Avoid the use of all chemicals and drugs* that are not absolutely necessary for sustaining life. They will severely interfere in the detoxification process and may be even more harmful to your pet during this time. As the curative process moves deeper into the constitution, the body may react even more than usual to these substances, possibly causing a reaction.

- *Avoid giving a vaccine booster* within six weeks prior to or after this type of detoxification. Shortly after a vaccination, the body will have a harder time detoxifying. If the detoxification is completed before a vaccination, the body may react more strongly to the vaccination.

- *Address symptom aggravations gently* through the use of nutritional supplementation, homeopathy, flower essences, or herbs. This will allow the cleansing process to continue, while keeping the symptoms subdued.

- *Keep track of your pet's progress* to help you understand the process they are actually going through. If you jot down a few notes each day, you will be less likely to be afraid and scare yourself into thinking that it has been "days" since your animal last ate, when in fact it may have been two meals.

If a discharge started three days ago and was clear but has turned yellow, you will need to add natural antibiotics such as garlic or echinacea to fight off any possible infection. Then you will want to keep track of how many days the discharge stays yellow, or how quickly it responds to the garlic or echinacea. You may want to seek out other support if necessary. On the other hand, if you noted that the discharge took two weeks to clear up and then returned in three weeks, but took only four days to clear up this second time, and did not return for two months the third time... then you will begin to see a pattern which indicates you are on the right track!

Each time the body experiences a curative response which has been supported and not suppressed, it gets stronger and the symptoms return less frequently and less aggressively until the symptoms are reversed completely.

WHAT TO EXPECT DURING DETOXIFICATION AND REBALANCING

Detoxification is the process of dumping waste. Therefore, waste will be present during the process. This includes, but is not limited to, the aggravation of the very symptoms you are trying to address by starting this cleansing process. This is a good sign! This *curative response* is a clear indicator that the body has been stimulated into cleaning itself by whatever detoxification protocol you are following. When this response occurs, many people become frightened and run to their veterinarian to get a drug to suppress these symptoms. This is the worst thing they could do at this time.

It is vital that these symptoms be supported rather than suppressed. If you choose to suppress these symptoms with holistic animal care or drugs, you will force the underlying imbalance even deeper. Chemicals or medications at this point, especially steroids and antibiotics, will severely burden the body. At the very least, you will have prematurely terminated the cleansing process through fear. But realize that this means that you and your pet will eventually have to go through the process once more if you can ever hope for true healing. It is best to address the symptom gently and naturally while continuing the detoxification process. Many things can be done to minimize the curative response without suppressing the cleansing and strengthening process.

Please note that it is more common for the process to happen relatively easily for most pets, regardless of their previous conditions.

Dogs who seem balanced and healthy prior to detoxification may exhibit the worst symptoms during detoxification. This response may come from a former imbalance that was suppressed. You must be aware of your own pet's individual process and support that, no matter what preconceived notions you may have had regarding what the process should be like.

ADDRESSING COMMON CURATIVE RESPONSES

Curative responses are a natural part of the cleansing process. It is vital to the ongoing strengthening of the body *to support these symptoms rather than suppress them*. The safest, most effective way to support symptom aggravations is through the gentle modalities of nutritional supplements, homeopathy, flower essences, and herbs. Please do not forget the power of love, play, and contact. Spend time nurturing your pet. It will certainly help minimize any stress they may be experiencing during the curative process.

Holistic Dog Care

Now that you are giving your dog a sound foundation—supported by love, behavioral guidance, daily exercise/play, proper nutrition with supplementation, and regular detoxification—you may want to explore how to prevent or reverse genetic and chronic disease. If your pet has an imbalance manifesting in a particular symptom, natural remedies can help. Herbs and homeopathy are also wonderful tools in supporting the immune response and curative process for both acute (sudden) or chronic (long-term) illness. Proper examination and quick response to changes can turn around a serious problem before it has a chance to become a chronic symptom.

TEN-POINT HEALTH CHECKLIST

I have prepared a ten-point checklist so that you can quickly identify and address any weakness or imbalance when it occurs in your dog. Always have this information available for the next time you visit your veterinarian, as it will help them assess the situation correctly. (See "How to Be Your Vet's Best Friend.")

1. **Nutrition**—What type of food do you feed your dog? How often do you feed your dog? Is her diet well-balanced? Bring in the label, if needed. Has your pet's eating habits recently changed? Does your pet seem satisfied, or is she always hungry? Has your pet's diet changed recently? Has her food possibly gone rancid, due to age or heat? Have you introduced any new supplements, treats, chewable toys, or food that may be creating the problem?

2. **Digestion**—Does your pet have daily bowel movements? Is flatulence a problem, and when does it occur? Before eating

or after? In the morning more than at night? Has the smell, volume, color, or consistency of your dog's stool changed recently?

Major signs of illness can include vomiting, diarrhea, or constipation for more than twenty-four hours. Pancreatic imbalance (fatty, discolored stool) and parasitic infestations (rice or string-like bodies within the stool) can be quickly identified by noting such changes in stool and pursuing a clinical diagnosis. These imbalances are then much easier to reverse, before they develop into more serious conditions, such as diabetes or irritable bowel syndrome.

3. **Urination**—Do you allow free access to a potty area, or do you impose potty times around your own schedule? Have you recently changed this potty arrangement? Does your dog refuse to use the same potty area as before? Has your pet's daily intake of water changed? Is his urine painful, scant, or bloody? Is there a metallic or sweet odor to it? Has your pet recently become incontinent?

4. **Skin and Coat Condition**—Has there been a change in your dog's sheen or general coat condition? Dry flakes, dull or greasy coat, hot spots, or pimples? Excessive shedding, hair loss, scratching, licking, fur pulling, etc.? Coat and skin condition can be a primary source of health-related observation, especially for symptoms involving the liver or kidneys. Toxic waste will often be eliminated through the skin if these organs are not kept in peak condition.

5. **Ears** can become inflamed or have a waxy discharge as the first signs of immune imbalance or toxicity. Have you seen pests, such as mites (small dark specks like pepper), for months prior to the immune system taking a serious dive? Allergies, yeast, or bacterial infections will often first manifest themselves in the ears. Are your pet's symptoms related

to allergy seasons or weather changes? Summertime pool play can create "swimmer's ear" in dogs as well as in humans.

6. **Eyes and Nose** may become inflamed along with the ears. Irritated eyes can create blocked tear ducts, manifesting in nasal discharge and respiratory difficulties. Have the infected eyes quickly become matted and painful? Is the discharge chronic? Or seasonally related? Red, swollen eyes are often symptomatic of improper liver function and detoxification. Genetic conditions, such as turned-in lashes, can be addressed early on before they cause permanent damage and even blindness.

7. **Nervous System, Bones, Joints, and Muscles**—Has your pet recently shown signs of confusion, lethargy, or uncontrollable shaking? Difficulty drinking or eating? Any rapid weight changes? Has her gait or movement, especially getting up or down, changed? Is there noticeable pain or limping? Restless sleep or exhaustion? Is there any body odor or fever present? A dog's normal temperature is 100° to 101.5°. Use a digital thermometer for one minute.

8. **Respiratory and Cardiac**—Has your pet's breathing changed? Can he play as long as he used to before becoming winded? Has he developed a cough or wheezing? Have his resting pulse rate or breathing patterns changed?

   Normal Heart Rate/Pulse: Take this inside the thigh on femoral artery.

   Small dogs—90 to 120 beats per minute.

   Large dogs—65 to 90 beats per minute.

9. **Emotional and Behavioral**—Has your pet recently become withdrawn, fearful, nervous, or aggressive? Has she become more destructive: chewing on herself, the furniture, or the walls? Has she suddenly begun soiling in the house? There can often be a physical problem behind these behavioral issues—just as stress can lead to health problems. Have

you or your family recently gone through a divorce, moving, death (of a person or another pet), or other stressful events?

Your pets will surely suffer the increased stress in their environment, much the way humans do. Often, they suffer more. All they are capable of understanding is that there is a problem. They can't fathom the cause of the change, or that it may soon be resolved—they just worry about it and the fact that you, as the center of their universe, are now different in a negative way.

10. **Environment**—Have you recently sprayed the yard for weeds or have you applied chemical pesticides in the house, yard, or even directly to your pet? Is your dog wearing a chemically based flea/tick collar? Are there any other poisons, radiator fluid, or toxic plants, such as poinsettias, available to your pet to chew on or ingest in some way? Have you installed new floor covering that might be seeping formaldehyde, or other toxins that your pet is directly exposed to? Has the quality of your pet's drinking water or diet changed? Has he been given a new medication or recent vaccination?

All of these factors can trigger a toxic reaction, weaken the immune system, or cause an organ failure. With ninety percent of pets' health problems today created by the toxic environment, it is vital that you become aware of what your pet is exposed to, or ingesting.

EARS, EYES, AND THE RESPIRATORY SYSTEM

Ear Problems can be the first sign of dis-ease, so it is important that you carefully check and clean the ears often. Early detection of parasitic infestation or bacterial and yeast infection can help prevent the spread of disease into the sensitive middle and inner ear. A healthy ear should be free of odor, discharge, or oily debris, and have clear skin tone with no irritation or discomfort.

Symptoms commonly occur in toxic pets. Also, many breeds have long, floppy ears that encourage a build-up of debris. Some breeds are genetically prone to ear problems, regardless of ear construction.

The liver, a primary organ often affected by allergens or toxins, is considered "in relation" to the ears and eyes. As the liver becomes burdened, the ears begin to exhibit symptoms associated with allergy problems and become more prone to irritation from grasses, pollen, and molds, as well as from foods and chemicals.

In addition, symptoms often occur during warmer weather when dogs are exposed to more bathing and swimming. Water can become trapped in the ear channel, encouraging bacteria and yeast to grow there, resulting in ear infections. Foxtails and other foreign bodies can also become lodged in the ear, triggering irritation and discharge. Always check first to see if you can find anything in your dog's ear and remove it prior to treatment. If needed, seek proper removal by a veterinarian.

Ears can be effectively cleaned with a homemade solution of two ounces of distilled or purified water, one teaspoon *Witch Hazel*, one teaspoon white vinegar, and six drops of *Calendula Extract*. Add an additional six drops of *Golden Seal Extract* if infection is suspected. Use a cotton ball to squeeze a little of this solution into the ear, rubbing the outer base of the ear and massaging the solution into any debris that needs to be removed. You may hear a slight suction noise inside the ear. Allow your dog to shake out her ear, then wipe out the rest of debris and fluid with a soft tissue wrapped around your finger. Do not insert anything down into the inner ear.

Rather, let the tissue absorb any impurities. Follow these cleanings with a light application of *Calendula Extract*, *Aloe Gel*, or *Vitamin E*. Use *Hypericum Cream* around the ear flap and opening if pain is present.

Be careful not to use heavy oil-based ingredients or vegetable oils, unless you want to dissolve a foreign body or kill ear mites. Although these products may seem to condition the ear and reduce irritation, the oil may nurture a bacterial or yeast infection by providing a warm, moist, oxygen-free environment.

For dogs with ear flaps in the down position, tie them up over the head with an elastic hair band to encourage air circulation. Doing this as little as one hour a day—possibly while the both of you are taking a walk—can aid the reduction of bacterial or yeast growth and encourage healing.

To dissolve a suspected foreign body which is not creating severe pain or bleeding, warm up two tablespoons of garlic-flavored cooking oil (to help discourage bacterial growth), or use soybean oil to which you have added a capsule of *Garlic Extract* with six drops each of *Golden Seal* and *Mullein Extract*, and 200 IUs of *Vitamin E*.

Apply with a dropper, spoon, or cotton ball, dripping it down into the ear. Allow it to remain there for as long as your pet will tolerate it. Finish by massaging the base of the ear to further loosen the object before flushing the ear out with the cleaning solution. Repeat several times per day until the object is removed, usually within a day or two. This will dissolve any hardened debris as well as any plant particles. Never force fluid into the ear with pressure, or you may drive the object further in, making it harder to remove safely.

If the ear seems more irritated, begins to bleed profusely, becomes unbearably painful, or develops a severe discharge, or isn't responsive within a few days to home treatment, seek out veterinary care immediately. Do not take ear problems lightly, as chronic inflammation and infections can lead to permanent damage, resulting in hearing loss. Reliance on chemically based, medicated ear washes or drops can also permanently damage the sensitive tissues of the ear, resulting in increased production of oily discharge.

Grapefruit Extract ear drops can also be applied after cleaning to fight bacterial and yeast infections. *Mullein and Garlic Oil* ear drops are also excellent for irritated and infected ears.

Avoid alcohol-based products, which can irritate the ears further. If you suspect water is trapped in the ear channel, a few drops of pure alcohol can dry up the water residue. Don't worry about the alcohol found in any herbal extracts you might be using—only insignificant amounts of alcohol remain in the final dilution. Unless your dog is sensitive to alcohol, avoid glycerin-based herbal extracts—I have found them to be less therapeutically potent in most applications than their alcohol-based cousins.

Proper grooming is beneficial in keeping ears free of infection or waxy build-up. Many breeds, such as Poodles, Terriers, and Cocker Spaniels, grow hair close around the ear and sometimes even in it. You must pull the hair out from inside the ear and clip the outer areas close in order to help the air circulate. Many dogs most prone to ear infection have a closed ear flap rather than a standing ear flap. This does not allow additional air to circulate inside the ear, which soon becomes a moist breeding ground, encouraging infection.

Ear Mites or Otodectes are tiny white spider-like pests, practically impossible to see with the naked eye. They leave a trail in the ear of digested blood and debris resembling finely ground pepper. A gritty discharge results. Chronic infestation can result in hearing loss. (See Immune System Dysfunction.)

To dissolve a suspected infestation (which may not create severe pain or bleeding), warm up natural ear oil and apply it as directed for removal of foreign objects. Allow it to set for as long as your pet will tolerate it, at least for one-half hour to dissolve any debris. Then flush the ear out with a cleaning solution. Repeat several times per day until all the mites are removed and symptoms are reversed, usually within a day or two.

Eye Problems are almost always involved in toxicity or sensitivities, often accompanying ear symptoms. (The condition of the ears and eyes are considered indicative of liver function.) As allergens and toxins burden the body, the liver may become overwhelmed. Resistance to airborne sensitivities in particular is then compromised further. Be sure to check your pet's eyes daily, wiping away any matter present. Always address eye problems quickly, as chronic irritation or infection can permanently damage the eye, possibly leading to cataracts, corneal ulceration, and even loss of sight.

To clean away slight discharge, use a warm, damp cotton cloth. Always use distilled water and wipe in the direction of the eyelashes to avoid further irritating the eye. Start in the inside corner, and allow your pet the chance to close his eye before gently wiping downwards towards the outside corner.

To remove heavy matter or copious discharge in and around the eye, use a warm, wet cotton pad or ultra-soft cotton paper towel. Hold it gently against the eye, allowing it time to soften any hardened matter. Gently wipe the inside of the lid to remove discharge on the eyeball, being careful not to introduce any dirt or crust into the eye. Then remove the remaining matter on the outside lashes. Repeat as often as needed. Do not allow the eye to remain crusted-over and shut. This will encourage infection, possibly damaging the eye or tear duct permanently.

Follow cleaning with an application of natural eye drops made from a dilution of six drops of *Calendula Extract* into a couple of ounces of distilled water. For very irritated or dry eyes, add 200 IUs of natural *Vitamin E Oil* to the eye drops, shaking the solution well before each use. Or apply a few drops every other day, directly to the inside of the lower eyelid, being careful not to scratch the eye. Blinking will disperse the Vitamin E. A few drops of *Golden Seal Extract* can also be added to eye drops, if infection is present (See Immune System). This will also help to open up tear ducts and to encourage natural lubrication.

Always supplement with herbs to strengthen and cleanse the eye, to increase resistance to allergens and infections, and to support successful anti-inflammatory and antihistamine action. Proper nutritional and herbal supplementation can prevent and even reverse cataracts—a common side effect of chronic eye irritation.

Cataracts also occur frequently in pets suffering from chronic problems (not necessarily related to the eyes), suppressed with frequent chemical treatment. Cataracts are a direct result of irritants and toxins from environmental and dietary sources that damage sensitive eye lens tissues, causing them to "scar" or cloud up.

A lack of assimilated nutrients such as *Vitamins A, E,* and *Zinc* (often depleted during chronic illness) can also encourage the formation of cataracts. Along with proper nutrition, I have successfully reversed cataracts with homeopathic *Silica 200C daily* for four weeks, then *Silica 1M weekly* for four weeks, then *Silica 10M weekly* for four more weeks. These higher doses of Silica should be used under the supervision of an experienced practitioner.

Corneal Ulcers are frequently seen in dogs who have suffered from inhaled, ingested, or environmental allergies. Lack of tears, scratching, and rubbing of the eyes, as well as nutritional deficiencies, contribute to the development of ulcers on the outer protective layer of the eyeball. Once your veterinarian has diagnosed this problem, it can often be quickly reversed with twice daily applications of natural *Vitamin E* (d-Alpha, *not* dL-Alpha) directly to the inner eyelid, so blinking can spread it over the entire eye. When there is no tear production or a blockage in the tear ducts, apply a high-quality, natural tear solution to prevent drying.

Upper Respiratory Problems can be the most frequently seen chronic symptom. The lung and nasal tissues can easily become triggered by environmental pollutants including second-hand smoke. Damaged from chronic wheezing and discharge, these tissues become even more sensitive. Daily cleaning of the nostrils, with a warm, damp cloth to keep the discharge and crusted mucus clear of the nasal passages will help facilitate healing. Homeopathic *Spongia* is a wonderful expectorant and lung toner. *Lobelia* is a standard herb for improved lung function. Other homeopathic and herbal supplementation can successfully address more specific respiratory symptoms.

TEETH AND GUMS: PROPER DENTAL CARE

Diseases of the mouth often revolve around gum problems (gingivitis), abscesses, and bad teeth. Proper oral care is vital to good health. Poor teeth and painful gums can contribute as much to your pet's poor health as chemicals can. When proper chewing becomes difficult, the digestive process begins poorly. Food gets swallowed whole and is more difficult to break down further for assimilation. Vital nutrients are lost, regardless of how good the diet is.

If chewing is too painful and your dog refuses to eat, the lack of food can quickly exacerbate an immune weakness. I have seen too many dogs starving to death because of bad teeth. Bacteria, which flourish in the warm, moist environment provided by the mouth, feed on the yeast and sugar in a dog's diet, and can trigger a severe systemic infection if not addressed.

Weekly cleaning of your dog's mouth, a high-quality dry kibble (home prepared, if preferred), chew toys (no rawhide), and bones will keep the teeth free of tartar. Chemical-based diets or treats for tartar control may keep the teeth white, but may prompt kidney or liver failure. These are growing quite popular, but I suspect that these chemicals will prove to be just as burdensome as others. Proper maintenance is the best, safest route to take to ensure that your dog's teeth won't be the cause of disease or death.

Examining and Brushing Your Dog's Teeth

To prevent tooth decay and oral problems, examine your dog's teeth weekly. Check for any signs of redness, ulceration, or discharge between the teeth and around the mouth and tongue. Note any cracked or chipped teeth and check to see if they are secure in the gums. See your veterinarian immediately when you observe abscessed, cracked, loose, or dangling teeth.

Follow this weekly examination by a brushing with a child's toothbrush for smaller pets and soft adult toothbrush for dogs over fifty pounds. If your big dog has problems opening her mouth wide enough, then a child's toothbrush can easily reach the back molars. You can also wrap a thin wet washcloth around your index finger to rub the teeth clean, which some pets might like better than a toothbrush, especially in the beginning. It takes a little time for them to get used to a toothbrush. Apply a small amount of natural toothpaste; adult or kid's is fine as long as you avoid fluoride. If you suspect a gum infection, use a toothpaste that includes *Tea Tree*, *Grapefruit*, or *Golden Seal Extract*. I prefer this to doggie dental paste, which can be full of chemicals, sugars, and artificial flavors.

Start the toothbrush at the back of the mouth and work your way to the front teeth. Try to open the mouth slightly so you can get behind the teeth and to the back bottom molars, a prime decay area. Wipe away any left-over toothpaste with a wet cloth. You do not need to use a lot of toothpaste to begin with, so there should not be much left over to wipe away.

I keep a glass of clean water in which to rinse the brush and then apply the clean brush *with water in the bristles* to scrub away whatever toothpaste remains between the teeth. It is safe for your pet to swallow a little of the natural toothpaste. Many actually enjoy the taste, but do not overdo it. You don't need to foam up the dog's mouth to get it clean. Pets don't like the foam and will fight you.

For any accumulated tartar that brushing has not removed, use a dental scraper available in many pet catalogues.

You can remove heavy tartar by applying a flat-edged scraper to the crown of the tartar build-up (at the gum line) and flicking it downward. It will usually just come off in a large chunk. Try not to allow your pet to swallow these chunks if possible. Once the majority of tartar has been cleaned, weekly brushing and proper diet should keep them tartar-free and pearly white.

As a side note, many people have begun to floss their pet's teeth, a practice I highly recommend. Always approach your pet gently when introducing anything new, even the brushing. Start by getting him used to having you rub a clean finger over his teeth and gums. Once your dog has become comfortable with this, you can proceed to brushing with toothbrush and floss in hand. Never force your pet to do anything or they will only fight you and then avoid you. Instead slowly introduce a new method. Use a "rescue" or calming flower essence remedy if needed.

Yearly teeth cleaning under anesthesia (animals are actually put on breathing tubes, as they would be during major surgery) may weaken your pet's immune system and interfere with their good health. Many pets had a reoccurrence of various chronic symptoms shortly after having their teeth cleaned under gas. There is always the risk of dying during any surgical procedure. Your dog should be put under anesthesia for life-threatening conditions only, not for elective procedures.

Most problems can be prevented, but, if needed, oral problems generally respond well to home care:

- *Bad breath* is mainly associated with poor dental hygiene. It is true that infected teeth sometimes will smell bad, but I have found that most cases of bad breath issue from the digestive tract, not from tartar build-up. If dental hygiene does not get rid of the offensive odor, be sure to detoxify and check which diet you are feeding. Brushing the teeth and the tongue will eliminate most of the oral odors, and the addition of a liquid chlorophyll breath product will also help temporarily mask the odor. Clean teeth and gums do not smell.

- *Painful gums*—Give a dose of homeopathic *Hypericum* a few minutes before cleaning. For gums that may be too sore to touch, apply *Clove Teething Gel* or standard drug store gel. Then continue with the *Hypericum* twice per day until gums are normal. *Mercurius* benefits irritable pets who have swollen gums which may bleed easily.

- *Gingivitis*—For gum inflammation, receding or infected, use a natural antibiotic rinse of six drops each *Golden Seal Root Extract* and *Calendula Extract* to two ounces of distilled water. Brush away any food with a wet toothbrush or cloth and rinse the mouth out daily after meals. This will act as an antiseptic, as well as stimulate tissue repair and rejuvenation.

- *Preventing Tooth Decay*—Weekly cleaning and basic nutritional support, as well as chewing products, will help. Avoid rawhide, which produces a sticky film that adds to the build-up on the teeth. Rawhide is a no-no on another count: It can cause intestinal blockage and death. Raw soft bones (chicken, pork, lamb, etc.) can choke your pet and also do damage to his digestive organs, but large, baked-hard bone or raw beef shanks or knuckles will provide a good surface to chew on. This helps to remove tartar from the surface of the teeth, as well as to stimulate the gums. Several hard natural and plastic chew toys have recently been developed for dental care. These are appropriate as long as they are made of good-quality, food-grade materials. I do not believe that these chew toys can do a proper job without a weekly cleaning. Several homeopathic remedies have been touted for tartar control. I have seen some success with *Calcarea Phos.*, both in a lower daily dose (10X to 3C) and/or higher potencies (200C), dosed weekly. But to be safe, keep brushing!

SKIN AND COAT CARE

Proper nutrition, exercise, and grooming will guarantee a healthy skin and luxurious coat. Most imbalances will first manifest as a skin or coat symptom, especially in allergy-related conditions. The skin, the largest eliminatory organ, can exhibit many symptoms. I will address the most common ones, followed by the homeopathic and specific herbal supplementation recommended. Supporting a healthy skin and coat condition starts from the inside out. Proper diet and supplementation will do more to prevent these manifestations than brushing and bathing could ever do.

Hot Spots, Pimples, Eczema, Cysts, Fatty Tumors, and Warts can be reversed with a combination of herbs including *Red Clover, Stinging Nettle Leaf, Cleavers Herb, Yellow Dock Root, Burdock Root,* and *Yarrow Flowers.* Together, these herbs help clean the blood and lymphatic system. They also improve a pet's metabolism by carrying more blood and nutrients to the cells and by helping in the elimination of cellular waste. This improved metabolism decreases irritation and scratching, while stimulating tissue repair. This combination of herbs is indicated for both greasy or dry conditions.

Apis, a homeopathic remedy, addresses rashes and the general irritation that prompts scratching or rubbing. *Thuja* and/or *Arsenicum* help reverse warts, cysts, and fatty growths. *Calcarea Carb* is an outstanding wart eliminator. *Silica* will eliminate growths under the skin, including cysts, abscesses, or ulcers. *Hepar sulph* is indicated for weepy, painful areas.

Greasy Coat or Offensive Odors can be additionally addressed through proper grooming (see Grooming), and a final rinse of one lemon (cut up, rind and all), boiled in one quart of distilled water for five minutes, then covered and simmered for twenty minutes, and left to sit in the water overnight. In the morning, strain the solution and refrigerate. Use this daily as a rinse. Allow it to air dry on your pet. You can spray it on irritated areas as needed. This lemon rinse has naturally occurring, antiseptic properties. You can add twenty drops of *Golden Seal* or *Grapefruit Extract* if needed for infection control. Homeopathic *Psorinum* is beneficial when the skin has an acrid odor with discharging pustules or hot spots that are slow to heal. It reduces production of the sebaceous glands, which are associated with a greasy coat and sebaceous cysts. In this condition, itching is aggravated by warmth, yet the dog is sensitive to cold and seeks warmth.

Dry Coat, Dandruff, Cracked Skin, and Thin Skin should be addressed with herbal formulas containing *Milk Thistle Seed* (for liver toxicity), *Yellow Dock Root* (for fatty acid metabolism), *Burdock Root* (for blood purification), *Echinacea Root* (antibacterial), *Sarsaparilla Root* (for disorders associated with hormonal balance), and *Oregon Grape Root* (for liver metabolism). *Arsenicum* is a good general homeopathic choice, while *Sepia* works well on irritations, especially cracked toes and feet that itch badly with no relief from scratching. *Psorinum* is beneficial when the dog's coat seems dirty and dingy, and is brittle and lackluster regardless of grooming. Topical application of *Jojoba Oil* conditioner can also help temporally to reduce dryness, while herbs and nutrients are building the body up and reversing the underlying imbalance.

Hair Loss, Poor Coat Condition, and Excessive Scratching are helped by a combination of *Turmeric Root*, *Black Catechu*, *Grindelia Flowers*, *Licorice Root*, *Ginkgo Leaf*, *African Devil's Claw*, *Yarrow*, and *Lobelia*. This herbal mixture protects the liver and aids in the detoxification of allergens, which may be at the root of the problem. This combination is beneficial when food allergies are suspected, especially allergies involving protein metabolism. Watch for excessive licking of the feet and legs (urea toxicity). Homeopathic *Arsenicum* is best suited for general hair loss. *Sulphur* addresses ringworm or other circular-patch irritations, which are often the cause of scratching and hair loss.

Excessive Licking and Resulting Lick Granuloma can be very frustrating to both the pet and the owner. Because the condition is not always accompanied by scratching, sometimes it can be left untreated for years, as long as it does not interfere with the owner's peace of mind. Once a hardened area appears—usually on the right paw along the liver meridian—it can become very irritated, even painful. Urea toxicity, caused by poor protein metabolism or poor protein-quality diets, results in a gout-like condition, which irritates the pet, who seeks relief through licking.

Licking—Excessive licking is not only irritating to the owner, but it will quickly exhaust the pet who will waste vital healing energy in the attempt to assuage the pain. Pets with long hair, or those who are shedding excessively, are also prone to hair balls and digestive upsets.

Although normal daily self-grooming includes licking the body clean, obsessive or chronic licking can lead to skin eruptions (see Hot Spots), and even growths (see Lick Granuloma). Homeopathic *Arsenicum* works best for constant licking, especially when a build-up of urea is suspected. *Apis* is for rashy skin. *St. John's Wort* and *Chamomile* help lessen the anxiety often associated with excessive licking. Try Flower Essences such as *Rescue* or *Mimulus*, which are good for obsessive behavior.

Lick Granuloma can develop on the body, especially around the lower legs and feet, after chronic trauma through licking has occurred. A hard knot will slowly develop within the skin, often becoming the primary spot a pet likes to focus on. It is commonly thought to be simply obsessive behavior and therefore is not addressed until the granuloma is big enough to see. Once the licking has become chronic, *it has also become obsessive behavior*, and must be addressed as such. Compulsive licking of the area, even if the "allergy" itself has been suppressed, will help continue the symptom cycle by re-irritating the skin. Although removing the granuloma surgically is often suggested by vets, I want to discourage you from doing this. Once the surgery is done, the granuloma can return stronger than ever and is more likely to become cancerous.

A combination of *Arsenicum*, *Silica*, and *Apis* (especially if the area around the granuloma is also swollen) sometimes will stop a lick granuloma from growing, and in many cases will reverse the site significantly. Once the site has appeared, *Calcarea Phos*, given frequently in lower doses, can reduce the licking and the growth of a granuloma (given additionally in a higher potency, weekly dose of 200C). I have never seen what I would consider the complete elimination of a granuloma. But I have seen a significant reduction (over eighty percent of the granuloma's mass) in a high number of cases, with the complete elimination of the obsessive licking.

Proper Grooming cannot be underestimated for stimulating waste removal (dead coat and skin), for parasite removal, and for supporting circulation (which will in turn bring more nutrients to the skin and coat for tissue repair). A daily brushing, followed by a rubdown with a damp terry cloth towel, can work wonders to maintain good skin and coat condition and to reduce shedding. Find a good grooming book to learn more about the proper technique and tools needed for your particular breed or mix. Avoid shampooing too frequently, as this can strip the coat of oils or can stimulate over-production of oils, resulting in a greasy coat.

DIGESTIVE AND GLANDULAR SYSTEMS

Digestive disorders, such as a lack of appetite, vomiting, stool changes, and hair balls, are the second-most common complaint I hear from dog owners. (Skin problems are the first.) Such disorders are a common reaction to food and other environmental toxins. They may be prompted by allergies and by reactions to chemical agents, vaccines, and pest control products. Digestive enzymes are commonly used to suppress some digestive imbalances. Although they can be beneficial, for long-term symptom reversal, you will have to address the actual imbalance.

Chronic digestive disorder symptoms can develop into more serious dis-ease, such as bowel, pancreatic, or liver cancer, diabetes, and bowel obstruction. Also, the non-assimilation of nutrients may lead to muscle loss and starvation. Holistic animal care can reverse these issues quickly and effectively. It will also help to prevent such disorders from ever occurring, by controlling and reversing accidental toxicity before the reaction becomes too severe.

Proper Feeding Guidelines

How you feed your pet is as important as what you feed her. Dogs fed only one meal per day often develop weight or digestive problems. The single daily meal puts too much stress on the digestive tract. It's far better to feed your dog half that amount, two times per day, allowing the body to digest and assimilate the food more thoroughly.

Puppies from weaning to four months should be fed four meals per day.

Sick dogs, or puppies, from four months to six months should be fed three meals per day.

Adult dogs should be fed two meals per day.

I do not recommend freestyle feeding, giving your dog unlimited access to food. Not only can they overeat, but you will be less likely to notice if their feeding behavior changes. Check every week to make sure that your dog is assimilating his food well and is sustaining his weight.

Use ceramic, glass, or stainless steel feeding dishes and water bowls: Your dog is less likely to develop a bacterial or viral infection. Such bowls don't scratch the way plastic ones do. Aluminum dishes can give a dog aluminum poisoning—dogs will chew off slivers of aluminum while they are eating, or you may scrape off pieces of aluminum while you are mixing the meal with a fork.

Provide plenty of fresh, filtered water. Never use tap water, which may contain contaminants. Be sure that the bowl is heavy and can't be tipped over. Also keep it cool and clean of debris.

Anal Glands can become impacted in dogs that are fed poor-quality diets and therefore have improper digestive function and burdened eliminatory systems. The resulting itching sensation will make the dog scoot their rear end across the floor and also chew at the area, which will become infected eventually.

Constant squeezing (or draining) of the anal glands may damage them so that they become impacted. I have found that many groomers and owners do not express the glands correctly, inadvertently creating the very problems they are trying to avoid. Please have your dog's glands expressed by a veterinarian. You should do this every six weeks at first, and then taper off until you can return to the vet once a year (if you feel it's needed at that time). If you feel comfortable expressing the glands yourself, use a lot of hot, soapy water to clean the area and soften the glands. It makes the job easier. A wet paper towel can help you get a better grip. Gently squeeze the glands at the base of the tail, until the waxy paste is no longer present.

Prepare this solution to encourage further drainage without squeezing: six ounces pure water, two ounces *Witch Hazel*, twenty drops of *Calendula Extract*, ten drops of *Golden Seal Extract*, and ten drops of *Yucca Extract*. Wet a compress with this solution and apply it to the glands without squeezing them. The compress will help eliminate the impaction and will also provide some antiseptic to the area. Rinse well with a fresh solution and follow with a topical application of *Calendula, Tea Tree Oil*, and/or *Aloe Gel*. Keep some of this topical solution in the refrigerator—it will soothe the irritated and inflamed tissues. Soak a cotton pad with the solution and hold it gently against the area for a few minutes—or spray it on—as needed. Repeat twice to three times a day until the swelling and redness is gone.

Apply *Vitamin E* and/or *Jojoba Oil* directly to tough or scarred tissue to help soften it. Avoid petroleum-based products, which will further irritate the area and encourage bacterial infection. These products can become poisonous if frequently ingested by your dog.

A few doses of *Homeopathic Apis* or *Hypericum* for irritation and *Arsenicum* or *Nux Vomica* for detoxification can greatly reduce discomfort. *Hepar Sulph* can help to reverse infected glands, although I have found it to be more effective when combined with *Arsenicum* or *Nux Vomica* and an herbal antibiotic such as *Golden Seal*.

Dried Chinese mushrooms, *Shiitake* and *Reishi*, when they are mixed with fiber-producing ingredients such as apple pectin, guar gum, or psyllium can help stimulate a complete evacuation of stool from the colon. This will keep the toxic waste from backing up inside the anal glands. *Astragalus Root* is useful for prolapsed conditions of the anus and for impacted anal glands. It works as a diuretic and will flush wastes, reduce edema, and promote the discharge of pus. *Garlic* is also indicated. Don't forget flower remedies, such as *Mimulus*, or a *Rescue* combination, if your pet refuses to allow you near him without a fight. (See Immune System.)

Appetite Problems, especially loss of appetite, can occur during curative responses. Check if your dog has a fever, and observe whether her fluid intake has changed. Either symptom indicates something serious is going on. Also assess your dog's level of stress, which can also interfere with appetite. Sometimes, a loss of appetite can have several causes.

For nutritional support, feed up to 100 mg. of *B-Complex Vitamins* per day, regardless of your dog's weight. This, in addition to a short fast (if you haven't done one recently), can quickly stimulate the appetite. Often, a lack of appetite is the result of a toxic overload.

Try a few doses of homeopathic *Arsenicum* (in general) and *Nux Vomica* (when the loss of appetite is accompanied by one or more of the following symptoms: nausea, vomiting, stool problems, or flatulence). *Belladonna* can be used for nausea, empty retching, and vomiting, as well as for your dog's refusal to drink water. A dose or two daily, *especially fifteen minutes prior to feeding*, can also help to stimulate appetite. Several flower essences, especially *Mimulus*, *Star of Bethlehem*, and *Rock Rose* or a combination act to minimize stress in general and can often settle a dog sufficiently so that it will want to eat.

Bad Breath is usually thought to be the result of poor dental hygiene and accumulated tartar. Certainly, you should rule out any broken, abscessed teeth or gingivitis (inflamed gum disease), and always care for your pet's teeth and gums properly. If this does not resolve the odor, address toxicity in your dog's digestive tract, which can result in a bad odor escaping through the mouth.

Old fecal material, poor-quality food, or by-products in the food that are not easily digested can result in what I refer to as "digestive composting." The lack of digestive enzymes and lack of water can also help the composting process within the intestines. Food backs up within the digestive tract, fermenting and breaking down slowly just like in a compost heap. The results are the same. When you turn over compost, you are releasing the trapped gases caused by naturally occurring organic decomposition. These gases can be quite offensive, as you probably have experienced if your dog has ever been flatulent (same process—rear exit). These gases are released from the digestive system through the mouth. If you try to get rid of it by cleaning your dog's teeth or handing him breath mints, the odor will return quickly. Homeopathic *Arsenicum* and *Nux Vomica* are excellent remedies for odor elimination. *Garlic* and *Parsley* work well to rebalance the digestive tract. *Garlic* encourages proper elimination and is antiseptic. *Parsley* or *Liquid Chlorophyll* will reduce garlicky odor as well as digestive swamp gas. If your dog's tongue is coated, detox her herbally and homeopathically for yeast over-growth. Use *Acidophilus* to replenish friendly intestinal bacterial—especially if antibiotic drugs have recently been used.

Bloat or Gastric Dilation is common in large, deep-chested dogs, especially in Great Danes, Irish Setters, English Sheepdogs, Standard Poodles, German Shepherds, Dobermans, Boxers, Labs, and Rottweilers. Some long-bellied dogs, such as Dachshunds, may also be more prone to bloat—particularly when fed only once per day or when put on poor-quality diets. Bloat is a gastric back-up of gases, resulting in a distended, bloated belly, accompanied by excessive salivation and rapid breathing. At the onset, dogs will be very restless due to pain. They may possibly try to eat grass. As the disease progresses, vomiting may occur. Severe constipation, weakness, and shock may set in. It is possible that without treatment the stomach may actually twist itself over and the dog may require surgery.

Improper diet and infrequent (once a day) or unscheduled feeding (at different times for each meal) will cause bloat more than any breed predisposition. Digestive difficulties due to soybeans and other poor-quality or inappropriate ingredients in commercial pet food can lead to a build-up of waste products in the form of gases. Flatulence is the first symptom an owner will notice, but it is often ignored until the situation becomes chronic and life-threatening. Genetically, all dogs lack an essential amino acid necessary to utilize soybeans properly as a protein. Soybean oil and tofu are acceptable, as they have already been processed and are more bio-available than soybeans, which have not been processed.

Prevention is the best cure! But in the event that your dog still gets bloated, homeopathic remedies can be life-saving. However, if within a half-hour of dosing there has been no relief, get to your vet immediately. If needed, dose on the way—it will not interfere with any clinical care they receive. *Nux Vomica* (for initial symptoms and anxiety and to prevent or reverse twisting of the stomach) and *Carbo Veg*. (for stomach distention with gas, possibly a bluish tint to the tongue and gums, and for shock) have been successful. They should be given together at fifteen-minute intervals until there is some relief, and then hourly until the attack is reversed. These two remedies will address the majority of indications.

For severe gastric stress with a painfully tight belly, a dry mouth with unsuccessful attempts to vomit, and shock or disorientation, *Nux Moschata* can provide some relief. For extreme, sudden bloating without the ability to pass gas, try *Raphanus*. For chronic conditions, *Arsenicum* (a general restorative), *Sepia* (especially if hard, dark stools are common), and *Belladonna* (with chronic, colic-like symptoms) can help prevent a reoccurrence. Use these remedies two to four times per day for two weeks, then taper off to one weekly dose for another month, while detoxification and dietary changes are implemented.

Colitis and Irritable Bowel Syndrome are common symptoms associated with toxins, especially yeast and other food allergies. The constant stress of other chronic conditions can also result in diarrhea, constipation (or both), mucous-covered stools, flatulence, and even slight blood in the stool. *Nux Vomica* and *Arsenicum* are a great homeopathic combination to use initially. *Phosphorus* helps to eliminate blood in the stool.

Digestive enzymes can also be appropriate, but I recommend that you limit their use to a few weeks at a time. The overuse of enzymes can imbalance digestion further. Calming herbs, especially *Wild Oats* and *St. John's Wort*, are also helpful.

Do supplement with a variety of bulk-producing ingredients, including whole grains, fruits, and vegetables, to stimulate evacuation and improve bowel functioning. Avoid psyllium, which may be too harsh when used alone. *Yucca* is a wonderfully soothing herb, as are *Aloe* and *Slippery Elm Bark*. If this regimen does not settle things, seek more specific support under each particular topic.

Constipation and Diarrhea are common symptoms associated with stress or toxicity. Some pets alternate between constipation and diarrhea, whereas others will have either one or the other. Constipation can weaken the body, due to the improper elimination of waste products. Rather than being eliminated, these toxins then continue to be reabsorbed through the colon into the blood. Diarrhea is often associated with food allergies. But I have also seen it caused by allergies or parasitic infections, which irritate the dog's skin, so that he constantly scratches or bites it—all that nervous energy just churns up the bowel.

Several factors contribute to bowel upsets, including medications often used during a crisis, such as antibiotics, steroids, and antihistamines. First eliminate any possible culprits, including:

- Hard-to-digest pet food ingredients, such as "plant cellulose," which is often soy castings, peanut shells, or recycled paper pulp
- Lack of exercise, especially with six hours or more of prolonged confinement
- Inadequate amounts of fluids ingested
- Excessive ingestion of fur due to licking and chewing
- Poor sources of dietary fiber (i.e., the paper pulp mentioned above)

Psyllium Seed or Husk is the most commonly used fiber to help regulate bowel movement, but often when used by itself, it can be too harsh on the digestive tract. I highly recommend combining it with fruits and vegetables and other fiber sources such as *carrots, apple fiber and apple pectin, guar gum* (a misunderstood but excellent source of natural fiber that swells to retain water), and *bran*. Chinese mushrooms, such as *Shiitake* and *Reishi*, have long been noted for their fiber content, as well as their curative potential in reversing chronic colon conditions such as pre-cancerous growths, which, when irritated, can trigger diarrhea. Cooked *oatmeal*, added to meals or given alone with vegetable, fish, or meat broth, provides an excellent source of fiber. It also has detoxifying properties to help eliminate old fecal material from the bowels. (See Fasting.)

Old fecal material can become toxic (especially with bacterial infection) and can push the body to eliminate the irritation, so that diarrhea results. Supplement with potent doses of a high-quality *Garlic* supplement (500 mg. to 1000 mg. per day for small dogs, and up to 2000 mg. for medium to large-sized dogs) for natural antibiotic support. Homeopathic *Arsenicum* (for general symptoms), *China* (for debilitating fluid loss), and *Nux Vomica* (for vomiting and/or appetite loss) are effective in relieving diarrhea and its associated symptoms.

Use herbal remedies like *Yucca* and/or *Calendula Extract*, *Liquid Chlorophyll*, and *Slippery Elm Extract or Powder* to soothe irritated intestinal tissues. Be sure that your dog's fluid intake is maintained, as diarrhea can quickly dehydrate her. Adding a half teaspoon of raw honey per twenty pounds of body weight per day to fluids or herbal preparations will not only soothe an irritated colon, but is also an antiseptic and will provide energy for a weakened pet.

Dehydration can be caused by excessive vomiting or diarrhea and will quickly shut down bodily functions, especially the body's attempt to detoxify itself when an imbalance of nutrients and electrolytes occur. To check for dehydration in puppies or small dogs, grab the skin from the back of the neck between your forefinger and thumb, pulling it gently upwards and releasing it. In medium to large-sized dogs, you can push the side of the lip up (like a sneer) and then release it—it should snap back into place quickly.

All such pulled skin should return to normal within a second or two. If it takes longer, the animal is dehydrated. If the skin remains in a peak and doesn't snap back, consult your veterinarian immediately for subcutaneous fluid replacement therapy. In all other instances you can easily rehydrate your pet orally with a feeding syringe or by encouraging fluid intake. Provide a minimum of one ounce of water per day per pound of body weight. Electrolyte solutions can be added to the water if the animal seems weakened by the dehydration or is constitutionally weak to begin with. Keep a dehydrated pet quiet in a cool, dark area.

Motion Sickness can be a behavioral issue. Many emotions, including fear, abandonment, aggression, or nervousness can trigger motion sickness. This is an acute reaction to motion in a car, boat, or plane. This includes *perceived motion*, the result of seizures or inner-ear imbalance caused by infections. (See Seizures; Ears.) Utilize an herbal combination of *Skullcap, St. John's Wort, Chamomile Flowers, California Poppy, Wild Oats,* and *Valerian Root.* These herbs will help to normalize and to restore the nervous system while providing a sense of calm, without the sludgy side effects of drugs. Homeopathic *Petroleum* and *Nux Vomica* are excellent anti-nausea remedies to be taken for travel sickness. Symptoms such as hysterical panting, excessive salivation, and restlessness, which commonly occur just prior to vomiting, respond well to a few doses the day before traveling: thirty minutes *and again* at fifteen minutes prior to departure, and again as needed during the trip. Flower combinations indicated for "fear" or "rescue" can also help reduce stress-related symptoms.

Stool Eating is a distressing condition where the dog, in an attempt to assimilate nutrients which did not metabolize correctly the first time, eats her own stool, and sometimes other animals' stool. Undigested matter remains within the stool and is smelled by the dog. Due to poor-quality ingredients and improper digestive metabolism, the body (monitored by the brain) thinks it is starving and orders the pet to eat more. Often stool is the only available source of food at the moment. Diabetes (where the blood sugar is off), liver or kidney failure (caused by protein loss), pregnancy, chronic dis-ease, or infection (caused by the need for more fuel) are often triggers of stool eating. Digestive enzymes, especially *Pancrelipase* and *Amylase*, can help to reverse the dog's need to eat stool. Herbs, such as *Dandelion Leaf*, *Peppermint*, *Fennel Seed*, and *Alfalfa* will encourage the proper assimilation of nutrients, while the homeopathic remedies *Calcarea Phos.* (10X alternating with 30C) plus *Nux Vomica* helps eliminate the urge.

Keeping the yard clear of stool is important when reversing this problem, since stool eating can simply become a nasty habit if allowed to continue. By the time the enzyme balance and proper assimilation are addressed, stool eating may have become habitual. It then needs to be addressed as an obsessive behavior. Sometimes, even when everything is in balance but when the dog is simply bored, he will begin to play with dried stools, which may lead to him eating them as well. Get toys—lots of toys!

ORGANS AND GLANDS OF THE DIGESTIVE OR IMMUNE SYSTEMS

Liver imbalance is often at the root of digestive and glandular disorders, especially those involving the immune system. It is vital that you are careful about what you feed your dog, as the liver can become congested and burdened. If you suspect liver dis-ease, immediately eliminate all yeast from your pet's diet and treats, and stop all flea relief supplements (garlic works better).

The liver is a primary organ of the digestive, eliminatory, and immune systems, which marshal the body's defenses against toxins, and are involved in tissue repair. The care and support of your pet's liver must be a basic concern if you are to be successful in supporting optimum health and wellness for your pet. The liver is responsible for a great deal of bodily functions—from metabolism of life-sustaining nutrients passing through the intestines, to detoxification of toxic chemicals, poisons, and drugs circulating in the blood. It is vital that the liver not be allowed to deteriorate or become stressed. Fluid can then build up within the abdominal cavity due to bleeding, resulting in anemia and pain. Liver congestion increases resistance to blood flow through the liver, starving it of nutrients and fluids. Luckily, the liver is remarkable in that it can rejuvenate itself, as long as there is some healthy tissue remaining.

I have seen animals come back from the brink of death after an accidental poisoning, as long as the liver was protected and supported during their recovery. Unfortunately, traditional medical care often overlooks the importance of liver support during illness, especially during a viral infection. Many puppies who have had Parvo and recovered *without* holistic support later developed liver disease. However, puppies that were supported holistically never suffer liver distress. Herbal supplements have proven helpful in rebuilding the liver. See the recommendations for maintaining a healthy immune system.

The Pancreas is a gland that causes digestive upsets when it malfunctions. It is primarily responsible for proper enzyme digestion of carbohydrates, fats, and protein. It is the place where pancreatic enzymes are produced and released, which then go on to mix with the other enzymes that will trigger digestion. Hormonally, the pancreas plays a vital rule in insulin and glycogen production. Improper pancreatic function can lead to several dis-eases, including diabetes and cancer.

Diet is the biggest culprit in pancreatic dysfunction. Chemical or viral exposure, parasitic infestation, and even trauma from a blow can also have severe consequences. Certain commonly prescribed drugs, antibiotics, and corti-costeroids can damage the pancreas or cause a malfunction.

Nausea and vomiting (especially of partially digested food), and fatty off-colored stools are primary symptoms of pancreatic malfunction. Loss of appetite, with excessive sali-vation and a marked pain in the right lower rib quadrant, can indicate pancreatic dysfunction. Dogs will hang their heads with their front feet bent out and their rear end in the air— almost as if praying—in order to relieve gastric pressure and pain. Pets who have been fed poor-quality diets containing rancid animal fats or meats, or those who have been allowed to become fat, can easily have a pancreatic flare-up. Rottweil-ers, Cocker Spaniels, German Shepherds, and Schnauzers are genetically prone to pancreatic problems, especially as they get older. Diet is the best way to prevent pancreatic problems, which are considered by most veterinarians to be *irreversible*. Continued use of toxic foods, chemical sub-stances, medications, and exposure to stress will lead to reoc-currence of pancreatic symptoms. General holistic care should be followed, and the secondary symptoms should be specifically addressed.

Diabetes is mentioned here because it is another disease that I can frequently trace back to a history of digestive problems associated with pancreatic dysfunction. I believe that the relation between blood sugar stabilization (or lack of it) and sensitivities resulting in digestive upsets has yet to be fully appreciated by veterinarians. I first perceived that many pets *finally* responded to medical treatment *for their digestive symptoms* only after they were diagnosed with diabetes (often later in their lives), and their blood sugar was stabilized through insulin and diet.

Adhering to a holistic animal care lifestyle when symptoms present themselves early in your pet's life will help prevent a diabetic condition from developing. Herbal support can also be very successful in reducing the amount of insulin therapy needed. I have seen a combination of herbs, in addition to proper diet and supplementation, wean many pets completely off insulin. A formula of *Devil's Club Root and Bark*, *Indian Jambul Seed*, *Dandelion Leaf and Root*, *Uva Ursi Leaf*, and *Turmeric Root* strengthens the pancreas, promoting better production and utilization of insulin. This herbal compound also normalizes and restores the organs and glands associated with carbohydrate and sugar metabolism, which are needed for curative energy. Re-synthesis of glycogen promotes the greater balance of glucose, and is indicated in both hyper- and hypoglycemia.

Spleen function is frequently overlooked or misunderstood. This valuable organ removes and destroys worn out, defective, or misshapen red blood cells, and thus reduces toxic build-up in the body. The spleen also harvests some antibodies needed in the fight against infection.

Adrenal Gland malfunction can be very common in animals who are exhibiting allergic reactions, especially chronic skin conditions. Frequently, this malfunction can be caused by previous cycles of corticosteroids, the very drugs that are most commonly used to suppress inflammation-related symptoms, including digestive upsets.

Cushing's Disease is a common condition associated with adrenal malfunction, specifically the overproduction of naturally occurring corticosteroids. This disease results in chronic symptoms, such as increased food or water consumption, frequent elimination, stress, intolerance of exercise, allergies, and reduction in muscle tone (especially in the belly). A pot belly is a symptom of this disease. This condition often includes skin lesions (pemphigus) resulting in thick, gray, leathery skin deposits resembling an elephant's skin. Within six months of natural support, this skin condition (presently believed to be irreversible) has been reduced in severity by up to eighty percent.

Addison's Disease is *hypoadrenocorticism* caused by inadequate amounts of circulating corticosteroids, the opposite condition to Cushing's Disease. Addison's Disease creates an imbalance of fluid and electrolytes, and can be life-threatening because decreasing levels of potassium and sodium will cause stress on the heart. Clinical symptoms look like gastrointestinal stress—vomiting, diarrhea, and dehydration. Problems with appetite and weight loss can be common, although water overconsumption might be present as well.

Herbal formulas containing *Siberian Ginseng Root*, *Chinese Schizandra Berry*, *Damiana Leaf*, *Kola Nut*, *Wild Oats*, *Licorice Root*, *Skullcap Herb*, and *Prickly Ash Bark* work well together to restore integrity to the adrenal glands, thus promoting greater energy and stamina, while building up the body's adaptogenic abilities against stress. *Astragalus Root* is a general herbal restorative for the adrenal glands. These herbs are nutritive and act as a tonic to the adrenals, the nerve cells, and tissue.

Homeopathic *Adrenaline* (epinephrine) is also helpful. Use this only in lower potencies such as 3X to 6X, and for no more than two weeks at a time, with a month off in-between uses. It is best used dosed with other remedies and supportive supplements. *Arsenicum* (for general adrenal malfunction, and secondary symptoms), *Iodum* (helps avoid stress on heart or skin), and *Silica* (helps counter improper assimilation of nutrients, reduces keloid growths on skin, and soothes anxiety) are all appropriate homeopathic remedies to use for adrenal support.

Thyroid Problems can be very common to animals with chronic skin or weight conditions. Cocker Spaniels, Golden Retrievers, Rottweilers, Dachshunds, German Shepherds, and Dobermans are very prone to thyroid imbalances. The thyroid influences metabolism, encouraging proper nutrient and oxygen utilization. Often, a glandular imbalance can be caused by previous cycles of corticosteroids and other immune-suppressive medications.

Hypothyroidism is generally the underlying cause of immune dysfunction, resulting in iodine deficiencies and underdevelopment or malfunctioning of the thyroid and pituitary glands. Symptoms include lethargy, intolerance of cold, dull coat, color change or hair loss, and poor appetite—often accompanied by weight gain, allergies, eye problems, seizures, and arthritis. *Hyperthyroidism* can lead to anxiety, obsessive behavior, or withdrawal and wasting disease. It can also lead to rapid weight loss due to muscle deterioration, regardless of strong hunger. *Yucca*, in the standardized extract form, seems to help the glands respond more quickly to nutritional support. *Sarsaparilla Root* is an excellent herbal remedy for the thyroid gland that helps to balance the hormones.

Use homeopathic remedies such as *Thyroidinum* (to rebalance thyroid function and address general symptoms); *Belladonna* (for thyroid toxemia, i.e., a pet who is easily excited, with general thyroid symptoms); *Calcarea Carb.* (for pets who are easily chilled, thyroid dysfunction with pituitary involvement, facial eruptions, or a flabby, distended belly with an aversion to animal protein and fat); *Spongia* (for gland enlargement, goiter); *Hydrastis* (for goiter, nervousness, and auto-immune problems related to thyroid dysfunction); and *Iodum* (for loss of weight and flesh, regardless of strong hunger).

Veterinary testing for thyroid or adrenal hormonal (cortisol) levels will benefit you in making decisions about your dog's care. Thyroid and adrenal gland function are fundamental to many wellness issues. Utilize medication only when appropriate for you and your animal, especially if nothing else seems to work. Long-term natural support can reduce or even eliminate the need for chemicals, and is safe to use in conjunction with medications.

Once you start on medication, it can be more difficult to eliminate the need to continue the drugs. Unless the situation is life-threatening, try holistic animal care first. Pets who have not responded to natural modalities are often diagnosed with deeper glandular malfunctions. Short-term medication may be all that is needed to stimulate the overall curative process.

There are many wonderful glandular products on the market today. I prefer *Glandular Extracts* (in powder or tablet form) to homeopathic ones, but please do not disregard a homeopathic combination with a potentized glandular *in addition* to a tableted form. Homeopathic glandulars work on a deeper level that is certainly beneficial to overall support, whereas tableted glandulars actually "feed" the gland directly and provide more substantial support in reversing glandular weakness. *Multi-glandulars* (a combination of several) are beneficial in supporting the weaker gland, but make sure that it is of sufficient potency in the particular gland that you do need to stimulate and support. Add another single glandular product to the multiple, if needed.

GENERAL SYMPTOM REVERSAL FOR DIGESTIVE DISORDERS

I have found homeopathy to be highly effective in reversing acute stomachaches, liver inflammation, and appetite or stool changes. It is also effective in relieving the underlying stress that often accompanies digestive disorders.

These are the homeopathic remedies that I prefer for digestive disorders:

- *Arsenicum* is used for digestive imbalances or general toxicity of the digestive system, and will take care of most symptoms, especially those with liver or spleen involvement, or after a season of chemical pesticide use (i.e., flea/tick control products, especially those with a monthly dose application).

- *Nux Vomica* also addresses the majority of digestive imbalances, including gas, vomiting, stool problems (especially alternating between constipation and diarrhea), or lack of appetite. It is a good complement to *Arsenicum*, especially when poor-quality food or chronic drug use is suspected.

- *Carbo Veg* is helpful when the pet is overweight, has chronic stool problems, seems to have trouble digesting well, and burps soon after eating. It is extremely beneficial when used with *Nux Vomica* in alternating doses.

- *Belladonna* is for the sudden onset of gastrointestinal symptoms. It can be used initially, then tapered off slowly and replaced with a more specific remedy. It is also indicated for acute colic and pancreatic imbalances resulting in a "fatty" stool.

- *Iodum* is for primary liver and spleen enlargement and pancreatic disease. The stool is whitish and fatty—frequently with a frothy diarrhea or blood. It is excellent for the anxiety and worry that is exhibited by a pet who is not fed soon enough.

Herbal remedies can support the prevention or reversal of many symptoms associated with digestive disorders. They can increase digestion or assimilation, and stabilize appetite. The herbs themselves are very nutritive as well.

Many pets cannot tolerate herbs on an empty stomach—in fact, the herbs may have been creating some of the pet's digestive stress. When pets have digestive upsets, it is best to give these remedies with a little food until the remedies are better tolerated. It also might be important to seek better-quality herbs. Poor-quality herbs or chemicals used to process cheaper herbal products may also trigger a reaction, no matter whether you give the remedy along with food or not.

Yucca Extract provides natural steroidal saponins, effectively reducing inflammation within the digestive system: the stomach, and intestinal lining, the thyroid or adrenal glands, as well as the liver, gall bladder, spleen, and pancreas. A reduction in excessive peristalsis (the squeezing response of the intestines to process and move digested material toward the colon) can help relieve diarrhea due to allergic and inflammatory responses. The intestinal pockets, ulcerations, and inflamed intestinal valves (that block passage of matter) that are often associated with colitis have also responded well to *Yucca* supplementation.

Garlic is a miraculous herb for digestive complaints. Not only is it an antiseptic and a natural antibiotic, it effectively supports proper digestion and colon health through its anti-parasitic and anti-yeast properties. It can be used to reverse flatulence, bad breath, general diarrhea, and fatty stool deposits.

Peppermint Leaf or *Fenugreek Seed* help reduce intestinal gas and cramping, prevent fatty deposits and colic, repair digestive tissue ulcerations, and fight infection.

Dandelion Leaf is an excellent liver and gall bladder tonic.

Siberian Ginseng Root stimulates the body's resistance to food or chemical sensitivities or allergies, and reduces fatigue and general weakness.

Milk Thistle Seed supports proper liver function and detoxification.

Calendula Extract contains therapeutic properties that address sensitive and irritated digestive tissues, including the stomach and intestinal lining, as well as the liver, gall bladder, spleen, and pancreas.

Cascara Sagrada Bark, *Barberry Root*, *Senna Leaves*, *Rhubarb Root*, and *Cayenne* are all beneficial herbs that effectively clean the intestinal tract. A detoxified colon is fundamental to rebalancing the digestive system and increasing the assimilation of nutrients necessary for proper health. These herbs can also prevent or reverse parasitic infestation.

Fennel Seed, *Ginger Root*, and *Anise Seed* can help relieve gas, cramping, and mucus, while stimulating proper digestion and peristalsis.

Immune System Dysfunction often gives birth to chronic conditions. It is the result of a toxic lifestyle and glandular imbalance. It is vital that you address and support your dog's immune function. Unfortunately, it is not uncommon to see pets develop a more serious dis-ease such as cancer in its many forms (organ, blood, tissue, or bone) years after struggling with chronic symptoms associated with poor nutrition, improper digestion, "allergies," reoccurring infections, organ problems, and arthritis.

Many people have reported the increased incidence or sudden development of cancer after their pet had been treated medically for another condition, such as a kidney problem. Although cancer is fast becoming the number-one killer of our dogs today, I still see it as a symptom and recommend that it be treated as such. The best way to reverse cancer and similar symptoms is to strengthen the immune system.

Vitamins C, A, B-Complex, and *E* cannot be surpassed for their immune-enhancing capabilities. Several other vitamins, amino acids, and minerals, such as *Zinc, Selenium*, and *Chromium*, will also enhance immunity. It is important to seek a properly balanced and therapeutically potent multiple supplement.

In addition, several herbal and homeopathic remedies can improve the body's resistance to allergens or infections, reduce catabolic waste (responsible for many skin and digestive symptoms), and eliminate damaged or mutated cells that often lead to the development of cancerous cells and a weakened immune response.

Herbal extracts, preferably organic and standardized (those with a stronger, guaranteed potency), should be diluted in purified water or apple juice and given on an empty stomach for optimum therapeutic response. If your pet is suffering from digestive disorders, herbs may be better tolerated when given with meals.

Immune-enhancing herbs include:

- *Sheep Sorrel, Burdock Root, Slippery Elm*, and *Turkey Rhubarb Root* is an old tribal herbal combination for eliminating catabolic waste and stimulating the immune system. Chronic cases often need this foundation for deeper detoxification and increased resistance to infection. Several breeds, such as Dalmatians, Cockers, Dachshunds, and German Shepherds, suffer chronic immune weaknesses and often fail to recover optimum wellness until after this combination is introduced.

- *Garlic, Echinacea*, and *Golden Seal Root* are nature's antibiotics, and have been proven effective in fighting off viral, bacterial, yeast, and fungal infections—while stimulating the immune system in general. This combination cleans the blood, lymph system, liver, and kidneys. *Echinacea* and *Golden Seal* can be used topically for the reversal of abscesses, gangrene, and pus. It also can open up blocked tear ducts.

- *Astragalus Root* helps tone and stimulate the spleen (an important immune system organ) to fight infection. It helps restore appetite, reduces fatigue, and lessens the diarrhea resulting from infection. It is useful for prolapsed conditions of the anus and impacted anal glands. It works as a diuretic to flush wastes, reduce edema, and promote the discharge of pus. It also increases metabolism and aids the adrenals.

- *Pau d'Arco* is beneficial for the whole body. It stimulates the immune system, heals wounds, combats infections. It also kills viruses, and is effective against cancers (including leukemia), lupus, cysts, and benign tumors. Use it both internally and topically for ringworm, hot spots, eczema, psoriasis, and staphylococcal infections. It is excellent for the general support and reversal of cystitis, colitis, gastritis, diabetes, and liver and kidney weaknesses. It relieves arthritic pain and is easier for very sick, weakened, or older pets to tolerate than *Golden Seal Root*.

- *Lomatium Root, Echinacea Root, Spilanthes, Chinese Schizandra Berry,* and *Licorice Root* in combination promotes strong anti-viral activity. This remedy targets cellular immunity and liver function to protect healthy cells from antigens and viral infection. It is especially indicated in cases of chronic viral infections that have not responded well to medications, or where the liver may be inflamed. It can be used with *Astragalus* for a debilitating or chronic infection.

- *Echinacea, Red Root, Baptisia Root, Thuja Leaf,* and *Prickly Ash Bark* as a combination acts as a blood and lymphatic drainer, while activating the body's immune response. It is a beneficial formula to treat a breakdown of the auto-immune system that is difficult to address. Other symptoms that respond well to this combination include anything manifested as a result of catabolic waste build-up: tiny blood blisters, pimples, mange, skin ulcerations, lymphatic engorgement, chronic infection, tumor growth, cysts, fluid cysts, cancer, and wasting disease.

- *Spilanthes Leaf and Root, Grape Root, Juniper Berry, Usnea Lichen,* and *Myrrh Gum* combined are very powerful anti-fungal and anti-yeast agents. These herbs have been proven beneficial in reducing Valley Fever spore infestation. This combination also helps the immune system respond to yeast overgrowth, vaginal infection, penis discharge, and ring-worm.

- *Echinacea* is good for irritated bowels and lymphatic engorgement. It helps address the fatigue often experienced during toxicity and subsequent immune deficiencies.

Homeopathic remedies can facilitate the immune system's response to a specific toxin, allergen, and bacterial, viral, or yeast infections, or parasitic infestation, although they should never be relied upon solely to address immune imbalance. If an animal is so debilitated, you may have no other choice but to use a homeopathic remedy. Otherwise, nutritional and herbal supplementation should be used as well. I have seen tremendous improvement in the immune system when I have included these remedies into the protocol.

Homeopathic remedies for immune stimulation include the following:

- *Arsenicum* quickly triggers detoxification and elimination through the liver and kidneys, and stimulates the other vital organs and glands that are responsible for proper immune response. *Arsenicum* also supports nutrient assimilation.

- *Gelsemium* is an outstanding remedy for the first signs of disease, especially fever. It is perfect for those pets who seem very needy and want to be held when they begin to get sick, and also for those pets who have had a relapse after a long, debilitating illness and a weak recovery.

- *Iodum* is appropriate for the first stages of liver, spleen, or pancreas disease. It is also beneficial for initial thyroid or adrenal gland dysfunction.

- *Sweet Chestnut* is a flower remedy which addresses the deep despair and anguish often experienced by a pet after a long illness. Flower "rescue" combinations should be used for overall support and immune stimulation when physical or emotional stress is present.

NEUROLOGICAL SYSTEM
Neurological disorders can be very frustrating to deal with. Many training problems and bad behaviors stem from an underlying neurological imbalance. Toxicity, either from

viral infection or chemical exposure, should be suspected in these cases, since the ensuing irritation to the brain and nervous system may quickly manifest in many symptoms. Damage to the nerves through structural or traumatic impact can result in mobility problems. Brain damage, from accident or blunt trauma, can trigger encephalitis (inflammation), resulting in seizures and pain. Even distemper and rabies, which are often fatal, have been successfully reversed using holistic care and can even be prevented through the use of holistic animal care and homeopathic nosodes.

Epilepsy (seizures) is now genetically common, especially among popular breeds or mixes of Chihuahuas, Chow Chows, Dalmatians, Poodles, Min Pins, German Shepherds, Labs, Cocker Spaniels, Dobermans, and Lhasa Apsos. It should be noted that all dogs are prone to epileptic seizures from ingested chemicals, viral infections, or trauma to the brain. I believe that yearly vaccinations, especially the aggressive puppy vaccination schedule, are more responsible for triggering seizures than the veterinary community is willing to acknowledge at this time.

There are so many other possible triggers for seizures, including sensitivity to yeast and urea, that I would suggest that we look deeper for a proper diagnosis. I believe that the usual diagnosis of epilepsy is often too freely determined, and pets are often unnecessarily drugged, leaving them prone to other diseases.

Epileptic seizure activity seems to be most active when the dog is resting. There is no set pattern or warning system. Some dogs suffer frequent fits, others more occasional ones. Heavy anti-convulsion drugs are often prescribed, which have debilitating side effects. Regardless of the cause, seizure activity can be reversed through a natural approach. Supplement with additional high-quality *B-Complex Vitamins*, *Vitamin E*, and the amino acid *l-Tryptophan* (1500 mg. daily—regardless of size).

Homeopathically, I have had success in reversing seizure activity with the following remedies:

- *Absinthium* addresses seizures that are accompanied by twitching and trembling, especially when preceding the fit, or when the fits are coming in small clusters.

- *Silica* addresses seizures which occur when the dog is resting or as the dog is waking up.

- *Belladonna* is helpful for the nausea or vomiting that follows a fit.

- *Thuja* should be used when vaccinations are suspected.

- *Arnica/Hypericum*, combined, works wonders in reversing seizures related to trauma, such as car accidents.

- *Bioplasma*, a combination of the twelve *tissue cell salts*, should be incorporated into daily supplementation for general support. You should add at least 100 mg. of *B-Complex Vitamins* per day, regardless of size, to rehabilitate the pet's nervous system.

Herbal supplementation can quickly reverse the underlying hormonal and stress-related imbalance triggering the fits. Utilize an herbal combination of *Skullcap*, *St. John's Wort*, *Chamomile Flowers*, *California Poppy*, *Wild Oats*, and *Valerian Root*. This combination will help normalize and restore the nervous system. It will also make the dog calmer and reduce the seizure activity, regardless of its cause. This formulation will not have the sludgy side-effects of drugs; indeed, it has successfully weaned many dogs off of the heavy narcotics used for seizure elimination. It allows them to live seizure-free *and alert* enough to enjoy their lives.

Encephalitis is the swelling of the brain caused by bacterial or viral infection, injury, or old age. It may trigger seizures and stiffness of the head. The symptoms are similar to those exhibited by dogs who have suffered from a stroke, and the recommendations are the same.

Paralysis or muscular weakness can be caused by a reaction to a specific agent—a viral, bacterial, or fungal infection, yeast, pollen, food by-products, chemicals, or medication. It may also have a neurological origin. Any of these causes may result in defective or damaged nerves.

After you get a proper diagnosis from your veterinarian, you can use nutritional, herbal, and homeopathic remedies to reduce inflammation, pain, and debility. Often a course of holistic treatment can result in complete reversal of reactive paralysis and a significant improvement in neurologically based symptoms.

Homeopathic *Aconite*, when given with *Arsenicum*, is the best remedy to use for the initial onset of paralysis. Give it in frequent dosages—it will provide initial relief of many symptoms. Taper off to two daily doses until recovery is complete. Use *Bufo* instead (or alternate with *Aconite*), if the initial onset follows severe arthritic symptoms. *Hypericum* is indicated when nerve involvement is suspected. *Carbo Veg.* is indicated for pets who *act* paralyzed, yet have no clinical symptoms (they have reflexes, etc.). This remedy is especially helpful if general symptoms of paralysis are preceded by chronic disorders and a severe acute flare-up.

Strokes can come on suddenly from a variety of causes. Symptoms can be minor at first, but the dog's overall condition can rapidly deteriorate. Often strokes become frequent occurrences until the pet is totally debilitated. It is interesting that strokes in dogs are very similar to those in humans. However, we do not know how much they are related.

The obvious symptoms are a pulling of the head to one side, droopy eyelids, and twitching. The dog may walk around in circles or get stuck in a corner and just sit and stare. Partial paralysis, especially of the mouth, because it makes eating and drinking difficult, requires more home care. *Aconite* is a good homeopathic remedy for strokes in general. Use *Bufo* if paralysis is the result of a stroke.

The best rehabilitative protocol for strokes is daily nutrients. Regardless of your dog's size, use *Vitamin B-Complex* (100 mg.), *Vitamin E* (200 IUs), *Selenium* (25 mcg.), and the amino acid *l-Tryptophan* (1500 mg.).

Rely on herbal and homeopathic remedies for other specific symptoms. *Yucca Root*, in the standardized extract form only, is as effective as corticosteroids in most cases where anti-inflammatory support is needed. *Yucca* can even be used in conjunction with steroids to reduce the need for heavy doses of this potentially harmful medication, until the dog can be weaned solely onto the herb for long-term maintenance.

HEART, BLOOD, AND THE CIRCULATORY SYSTEM

Anemia is a common symptom in chronically suffering pets. I believe that many cases of anemia arise from liver complications. Common symptoms of anemia include lack of stamina, a depressed appetite, poor coat condition with slow tissue repair, poor immune function, muscle weakness, washed-out gums, and dull eyes. Sometimes you can smell the faint odor of metal on the dog's breath. More serious anemia needs proper diagnosis and treatment, but border-line anemia is commonly reversed with proper nutrition.

Iron supplementation, a well-known treatment for anemia, will quickly reverse symptoms. Always use a good-quality source such as an iron proteinate (where iron has been chelated and combined with an amino acid) for superior absorption. Be careful not to overdo iron supplementation, as it can easily become toxic. The first symptom of toxicity is constipation. Limit daily levels to around 10 mg. for small dogs and 20 mg. for medium to large dogs. In addition, provide *Chromium* to help iron assimilation. It reduces the need for higher levels of iron. I also utilize *Alfalfa*, both in herbal (nutrient-rich) or in a lower-potency homeopathic form. *Taraxacum 30C* is also a good homeopathic choice as is its herbal twin, *Dandelion*.

Avoid feeding the dog liver meat on a regular basis. Although liver is a popular remedy for anemia, it is a primary detoxifying organ in an animal's body and stores many of the toxins it has eliminated from the blood. When you feed your dog liver, you are also feeding it concentrated toxins, including growth hormones and antibiotics!

Heart—Problems like a rapid heartbeat can accompany chronic allergy or arthritic reactions with powerful surges of histamine and adrenaline which stress the heart. Or such heart problems may be the result of years of improper diet and use of chemicals. Be sure to report any changes to your vet in your dog's breathing patterns, or any weakness prompted by exercise. If heart problems are diagnosed, nutritional supplementation with *Vitamin B-Complex*,

Vitamin E, Selenium, Chromium, and *Zinc,* as well as *Hawthorn Berries,* can help strengthen the heart muscle and regulate heart function.

Homeopathic remedies can quickly address acute symptoms, as well as stimulate an underlying reversal of debility when used on a long-term basis. Such remedies include:

- *Digitalis Purpurea* is indicated after an attack in which the pet collapses as the result of exertion, often with the gums and tongue turning blue. Generally the pulse or heart rate may be abnormally slow. There may be a history of liver problems and fluid retention. Use 10X twice a day for two weeks following an attack, then dose with a 30C weekly to reduce the likelihood of a reoccurrence. Many pets have lived years after a serious attack, with the help of this remedy. If needed for an acute attack, dose every few minutes on the way to the veterinarian (to help stabilize your dog).

- *Aconite* is beneficial when labored breathing and tumultuous heart action follows an allergic or emotional response, or when heart inflammation is suspected.

- *Iodum* reduces acute heart inflammation. It can be combined with *Arsenicum.*

- *Arsenicum* is indicated when weakness is triggered by a chemical reaction, particularly by vaccination, topical skin treatment, or pest control product. The heart may experience fluctuations between rapid and labored beating.

- *Calcarea fluorica* should be used as a regular tissue cell salt supplement, as it can strengthen a dilated heart with a weak pulse.

Heartworms are a serious parasitic infestation of the blood. This can be a fatal infestation, both from the heartworms that clog the heart, and from the chemical cure. If the drug's side effects don't kill the dog, the dead worms may block the heart so that it can't function. Prevention is definitely the best cure. Homeopathic nosodes (preventative and rehabilitative) have proven to be reliable. (See Parasites.)

Heart Murmur can be a common congenital defect, allowing some blood leakage from a heart valve, back into the atria under pressure. Many smaller breeds, especially the Poodle, Schnauzer, Lhasa Apso, and Shih Tzu suffer from heart murmurs. Proper diet and supplementation can reverse this weakness and repair heart tissue. Herbally, *Hawthorn* is an outstanding heart remedy. Homeopathic *Aconite* is a general heart remedy, especially for the valves and arteries. *Iberis* is indicated if pet is easily excitable.

Circulation is often slowed down by inflammatory responses, fluid retention, and heart conditions. Other than proper nutrition and detoxification, herbal *Cayenne* can greatly stimulate circulation.

Homeopathic remedies that work well on specific circulatory symptoms include:

- *Belladonna* has marked action on the vascular system—especially with pets who are often frightful or aggressive, or who lack appetite and stamina, or who are sluggish in general.

- *Calcarea Phos.* is an important tissue cell salt for poor circulation. Pets with poor circulation are often overweight. Their mouths and feet may feel cold to your touch.

- *Phosphorus* is indicated for any internal bleeding.

THE URINARY SYSTEM

It is very important to pay attention to urinary problems. Your dog has to have a proper diet and free access to drinking water. He has to be able to urinate when he needs to.

Holding urine in the bladder for extended periods of time leads to bacteria and crystal build-up. Urine flushes waste out of the body.

Urological Disorders are common in pets who have been fed poor-quality diets, given long-term medications, or who have suffered chronic dis-ease. As the body attempts to eliminate toxins, the urinary tract can become irritated and even blocked by bacteria or mineral crystals. Chemical poisoning or severe infection can further damage the kidneys.

Several breeds, especially Cockers, Dalmatians, and Schnauzers, are prone to kidney stone formation, as well as kidney disease in general. Low-protein diets are often the prescribed course of treatment. Yet this may actually place an additional burden upon the body. Because the body is losing protein due to the kidney disease (since damaged organs leak protein), it needs a high-quality bio-available protein. Otherwise, the body will turn on itself, and use its own muscles as a protein source. This accounts for the "wasting dis-ease" common with kidney failure. Detoxification can often clear up this chronic condition, but additional support may be needed. *Vitamin C* (a minimum of 1000 mg. per twenty-five pounds of body weight, per day) will acidify the urine, greatly reducing bacterial infection and kidney stone formation.

Herbal care can strengthen and tone the bladder and kidneys, encourage urine output, and eliminate blockages and infection. Try the following herbs:

- *Juniper Berry*, *Spring Horsetail*, *Corn Silk*, and *Goldenrod Leaf*, combined, can stimulate proper urine production and flow, eliminate toxins, reduce obstruction and stone formation, and soothe irritated membranes. The disinfecting properties of this combination will also help to reduce infection.

- *Usnea Lichen, Uva Ursi Leaf, Pipsissewa Herb, Echinacea Angustifolia and Purpurea Roots, Flowers, and Seeds* are very fast-acting and powerful antibiotics for urinary tract infections and associated cystitis and nephritis. Certain therapeutic agents are known to target the bacteria responsible for urinary irritation and inflammation. This herbal combination is safe for long-term treatment and crisis care in older or more debilitated pets. It can be used safely with prescribed antibiotics, and it is especially useful when weaning a dog off of chronic drug use. Use it to build up herbal properties while the drugs attack the more acute infection—when the drugs have been discontinued, the herbs will repair and protect the urinary tract to prevent the reoccurrence of the infection.

- *Yucca* is an alternative to steroids.

Homeopathy can quickly address acute symptoms:

- *Cantharis* or *Aconite* reduces irritation and pain urinating.
- *Thlaspi Bursa* can quickly promote the flow of urine in pets who, because of the accumulation of gravel, have been urgently straining. It can often replace catheter use. It is beneficial when uric acid builds up from improper protein metabolism, and when phosphates are present in the urine as a result of poor kidney function.

Incontinence is a concern of many dog owners, especially those who own spayed females. Urine leakage can be more common during rest, but loss of urine during excitement or toxicity can also occur. Herbally, *Plantain Leaf and Corm, Buchu Leaves, Corn Silk, Horsetail Grass, Arnica Flowers,* and *Thuja Leaf* work well to control incontinence by regulating and strengthening the musculature and organ function, by stabilizing hormonal balance, and by toning the membranes of the entire urinary tract.

Homeopathic remedies are very effective for incontinence. I highly recommend the following remedies:

- *Causticum* is indicated for paralysis of the bladder, and involuntary loss of urine during excitement or coughing. The pet may also be withdrawn, but will act abandoned if left alone. This condition often follows a long period of debility, medication use, and/or surgery.

- *Gelsemium* is for the pet who passes profuse, clear, watery urine from excitement or fear, yet seeks to be left alone. She may also suffer from diarrhea triggered by strong emotions or fright. She suffers from chills and may have bad breath.

- *Nux Vomica* is indicated in a pet who dribbles urine, often due to an irritated bladder or as a result of a poor-quality diet. The pet will seem to "feel the urge" too late. He can't make it outside in time.

REPRODUCTIVE ISSUES
Spay and Neuter—It's the Only Way!

I have heard them all: "We want to show the kids the miracle of birth." "He'll get fat and lazy." Or even better, "Ouch, that *hurts me*!" These are all misconceptions about altering your dog. What is known is that spayed females are less likely to have mammary or uterine cancer, are less likely to run off, and are more likely to be healthy and happy. Neutered males are easier to train (although no less aggressive), are less likely to suffer from prostate cancer, are less likely to run off, and are more likely to live a balanced, carefree life.

Neutering or spaying should not be used instead of proper behavioral guidance. Although aggression is a learned behavior, pets who have the urge to reproduce can be difficult to house train, may embarrass you in front of company, and will tend to run off, get into fights or car accidents—or worse, fall into the hands of someone who will abuse them, possibly selling them off to a lab or puppy mill (especially if your dog is purebred). I highly recommend surgical birth control as a life-saving measure.

A few doses of homeopathic remedies can help your pet quickly recover from the operation with few side effects. Use *Aconite*, *Hypericum*, *Arsenicum*, and *Nux Vomica* before and for a few days afterward, in frequent doses throughout the day to address many related symptoms. *Phosphorus* can help to reduce bleeding. Flower combinations for "rescue" are also helpful, especially if your pet is anxious. Having your pet inoculated during surgery can be detrimental to his recovery.

Reproduction can be difficult for pets who are toxic or who have suffered from chronic conditions. These dogs often cannot produce enough material (eggs, sperm, hormones, enzymes) to reproduce. I say trust nature and stop trying to get them pregnant. *A healthy dog will easily reproduce!*

Please do not breed any dogs with a history of poor health or emotional instability. It takes many generations to *breed out* a bad trait (if it is at all possible), so forget this angle unless you have twenty years and a lot of genetic research behind you. A trip to the shelter should quickly cure you of wanting to bring more puppies into this world, puppies who may never find a home, no matter how many friends you think will take one of them.

Pregnancy should be an easy process for both the mom and litter, if you and your dog are prepared. Proper care and support will ensure that everything will come out all right, and your pet will be better able to handle crisis if any problem should arise. Many pets first develop symptoms while they are pregnant. This is understandable, given the amount of toxins produced by supporting the growing litter. Some dogs never have a reoccurrence of symptoms after the pregnancy. However, it is not uncommon to find that a dog's pregnancy was the onset of her chronic allergies or arthritis.

Because many herbs can be dangerous during pregnancy, please avoid the following: *Angelica, Golden Seal, Pennyroyal, Mugwort, Wormwood, Rue, Barberry, Cascara Sagrada, Buchu, Juniper,* or *Ephedra.*

In the event that you suspect your pet is exhibiting symptoms of pregnancy, utilize a well-balanced nutritional supplement with a potent *Vitamin B-Complex* and *Vitamin C.* Also apply *safe* herbal remedies. You can rely on the effectiveness of homeopathic remedies as well at this time. You must expect the unexpected during your dog's pregnancy. No matter what you are doing, even if you have been doing it before for your pet, be careful, and keep a close eye on the mother-to-be for any reactions to stress so that you can adjust her feeding and supplementation plan before there is a crisis. Afterbirth and discharge should be dark greenish-brown and odorless. The discharge should clear up within a day. If it becomes putrid-smelling or thickens, apply the protocol for infections, and consult a veterinarian.

These are beneficial and safe homeopathic remedies for use during pregnancy:

- *Arsenicum, Apis,* and *Nux Vomica* are safe for detoxification, digestive upsets, excessive licking, scratching, and skin eruptions, or for the reoccurrence of old symptoms.

- *Pulsatilla* relieves reactive diarrhea during pregnancy, if your dog is highly excitable or suffers from exhaustion that is worse during the day. It is good for the elimination of the placenta after birth, and it boosts milk production. A general female restorative, *Pulsatilla* both promotes the flow of milk at birth, and helps to dry up the milk during weaning.

- *Phytolacca* promotes milk production and flow. It is useful when the breasts are hard and painful.
- *Alumina* is good for abnormal cravings, small, hard, knotty stools, or difficulty passing stools.
- *Phosphorus* helps reduce uterine bleeding. It will settle a bitch who gets anxious in the early evening and hides from her pups.

STRUCTURAL SYSTEM: MUSCLES, BONES, AND JOINTS

Arthritis is often used as a catch-all phrase to identify a wide variety of symptoms associated with muscle, bone, and joint disorders. These symptoms occur generally in conjunction with or as a direct reaction to certain conditions, especially those involving a congested or malfunctioning liver, kidneys, pancreas, and adrenal and thyroid glands.

Osteoarthritis is a common degenerative joint disease in which the cartilage is deteriorating or defective. *Hip Dysplasia* is a common form of degenerative joint disease. Many cases of arthritis are often caused by tissue damage rather than heredity. Improper nutrition, as well as old injuries from car accidents or physical overexertion can also cause these conditions. Infectious arthritis, with its joint inflammation and pain, is often caused by a fungal, bacterial, or viral infection.

Tick Fever, if left untreated, can permanently damage cartilage and joints. Fever and fatigue with swollen joints can accompany cases of infectious arthritis. Autoimmune disease can trigger arthritic conditions. The body turns on itself, and many antibodies bond together within the joint, causing inflammation. The smaller breeds, such as Toy Poodles, Chihuahuas, and Min Pins, are more likely to suffer from autoimmune-related arthritis, while *Systemic Lupus* (another autoimmune disease) favors the larger breeds.

The use of corticosteroids (anti-inflammatories) and pain medication may temporarily suppress arthritic symptoms, but will do little to repair the joints or to prevent further deterioration. Glucosamine, which has recently been touted as a revolutionary veterinary drug, is a well-known nutritional supplement. It is limited in its ability to help arthritis. Those animals who respond well, respond really well. However, fewer animals actually seem to respond than has been advertised. A dog must lack synovial fluid (this is what Glucosamine stimulates), and many joints, such as the hips, are not as strongly affected by a lack of synovial fluid. Unfortunately, many people feel that Glucosamine is the best available remedy and fail to explore others that are less expensive and that may work better.

Symptoms of arthritis and other structural conditions can best be suppressed *and possibly eventually reversed* homeopathically and/or herbally, while the joints, ligaments, muscles, and tendons are strengthened through nutritional supplementation. *Prevention is definitely possible.*

These following structural or muscular conditions also respond well to holistic animal care, often eliminating the need for surgery or anti-inflammatory medications:

The Cruciate is a knee ligament known for weakness, tearing, or severe sprain. It occurs in many dogs who have not been fed the best diet nor supplemented with adequate levels of *Vitamin C* (minimum 1000 mg. per day for small dogs, 2000 to 4000 mg. per day for larger dogs). Small breeds are the most prone, due to their structure and propensity for getting underfoot, thereby suffering injuries.

Hip Dysplasia, a partial dislocation of the hip joints, is genetically passed down in many popular current breeds including German Shepherds, Dobermans, Rottweilers, Labs, Golden Retrievers, Mastiffs, and St. Bernards. The genetic trait has become so dominant that in several breeds, particularly the Shepherds, as many as eight out of every ten pups born will develop symptoms before their second birthday. Severe trauma from a car accident, excessive exercise or jumping, and dog fights can also dislocate the hips. Avoid encouraging your dog to overexert, jump up too high or especially straight up and down, or rotate his or her limb. This sort of movement can damage the joint and tear ligaments. Never pull your young pup by the legs, and always limit their exercise until they reach twelve months of age, the age when a dog's proper growth has been reached, and its structural and muscular systems have been strengthened.

Most symptoms occur in the first six to twelve months of age. I believe that this is due to owners pushing their young pups, who may *look* grown due to their large size, but who have not really matured. Their young tissues are sensitive to trauma. The most common symptoms of hip dysplasia are walking with a great rear-end wiggle or bunny hop, and discomfort or trouble getting up and down. You must limit your dog's exercise to a few short walks per day. If the joint is pushed too far, to the point of fatigue, the tissue will begin to degenerate, resulting in inflammation and pain.

Avoid encouraging or allowing pups to run about too wildly, as this can trigger inflammation and pain. Swimming is an excellent way to exercise your dog while strengthening his ligaments. The stronger you can build the connective tissue, the more stable the hip will remain within the joint, reducing the damage which leads to joint degeneration, calcification (from chronic bone repair), and pain.

Surgery is often sought to stabilize the hip, but unless total dislocation has occurred, it is not effective in the long run. Nutritional, herbal, and homeopathic remedies have provided more support and recovery in a higher number of severe cases than I have seen through surgery.

High doses of *Vitamin C*, up to bowel tolerance, or at least 2000 mg. for smaller dogs to 4000 mg. for the larger breeds, can help to prevent hip dysplasia or at least to slow down the degeneration and to help relieve the pain. If surgery is needed, Vitamin C will help speed up recovery.

Legg-Perthes Disease is an orthopedic condition of the hips found in smaller breeds, such as Dachshunds, Terriers, or Miniature Poodles. It is characterized by the degeneration of the head of the femur where it fits into the socket to form the hip joint. This results in general lameness and pain with movement and upon getting up. Follow the recommendations for hip dysplasia.

Metabolic Bone Disease results in a thinning and loss of bone tissue. This leaves dogs predisposed to fractures, growth deformities, and bone cancer. *Hyperparathyroidism* is a common condition—a calcium deficiency within the bone leads to abnormal bone growth and tissue loss as the body tries to correct the calcium imbalance. This condition is associated with a high-protein or all meat-based diet, or follows kidney disease. These bone conditions increase the likelihood that your pet will suffer from bone cancer. *Boron* is a vital supplement for this condition. Herbs, including *Red Root*, *Thuja Leaf*, *Blue Flag Root*, and *Baptisia Root*, are helpful in reducing bone tissue loss. *Echinacea* stimulates and balances the immune system and prevents the infection from settling deeper.

Myositis triggers inflammation of the muscle tissue, resulting in stiffness, pain, weakness, and eventual muscle atrophy. Partial, short-term paralysis is not uncommon after acute bouts. Autoimmune disease, such as *masticatory myositis*, which affects the facial muscles and can cause difficulty in eating and drinking, is a common hereditary trigger in German Shepherds. Infectious states, including some parasitic infestation, can also trigger the symptoms, which are best treated individually as separate symptoms, rather than as a disease. Herbs, especially *St. John's Wort* and *Valerian Root*, can relax muscular stress. Massage and gentle exercise can also help strengthen the muscular system and greatly improve mobility and flexibility.

Osteochondrosis (Panosteitis: Hypertrophic Osteodystrophy, or HOD) is a common condition characterized by the abnormal growth and development of joint cartilage in young, large-breed dogs, resulting in lameness and pain. Overexertion and a high-protein, high-calorie diet are the most common culprits—although many parents may pass this predisposition along. It can be easily prevented by providing proper supplementation high in *Vitamin C* and *Boron*.

Patellar Luxation is similar to hip dysplasia, but it is localized within the knee. Improper nutrition has left the ligaments that surround and stabilize the knee weakened and vulnerable to injury or degeneration. (See Hip Dysplasia.)

The following homeopathic remedies are highly effective in reversing acute or chronic symptoms associated with bone, joint, or muscular disorders:

- *Arsenicum* is an excellent general arthritic and pain remedy.
- *Arnica* reduces swelling, muscular pain, and discomfort.
- *Bryonia* helps the pet who is stiff upon getting up and *cannot* walk out of it.
- *Rhus Tox* is for the pet who is stiff upon getting up but *can* walk out of it.
- *Hypericum* reduces nerve irritation and pain common in animals who are constantly licking their legs and feet, and sometimes even their backs.
- *Ruta* is best for severe tendon or ligament strains, common in nutritionally depleted pets. This homeopathic remedy has repaired the Cruciate ligament that is often severely damaged and torn enough for surgery, but in this case was still sufficiently attached to have tissue regenerated.

Herbally, I highly recommend the following remedies:

- *Yucca* is a very effective anti-inflammatory. Its stalk and roots contain steroidal saponins, which react in the body like chemical steroids, but without the side effects, to reduce tissue inflammation and pain. *Yucca* encourages a range of motion which will keep the joint from freezing up. Use a cold-pressed extract, rather than a powder or tincture. The extract contains up to eighty-five percent more bio-available saponins than other forms, and it is easier on the digestive tract.
- *Garlic* is a wonderful supplement for inflamed joints.
- *Milk Thistle*, *Licorice*, *Alfalfa*, and *Dandelion* are all excellent remedies for liver and blood detoxification. They can reduce the free radicals that may irritate joints.

Nutritionally supplement with the following:

- *Vitamin C* reduces inflammation, strengthen ligaments and tendons, and reduce allergy sensitivities. It is an excellent anti-oxidant and is the best joint and ligament vitamin.

- *MSM*, a sulphur-based product, reduces inflammation, and helps poor skin and coat conditions.

- *Anti-oxidant*s such as *Selenium*, *SOD*, and *Vitamin E* reduce inflammation.

- *Glucosamines* help replenish synovial fluid, an imbalance of which can create the rubbing of bone upon bone, resulting in pain and encouraging calcium build-up—the repercussion of which is worse arthritis.

- *Boron* helps with calcium absorption and strengthens bone density. It helps to avoid build-up of calcium or over-calcification, as found in arthritic conditions.

PARASITES

Parasites can seriously compromise the body, interfering with proper digestion and assimilation, and leaving the body more susceptible to imbalance and dis-ease. Parasitic infestation can be deadly: Infection can set in and organ failure can occur. You must keep your pet free of infestation. If you suspect *intestinal worms* because there are chronic stool problems, with evidence of mucous-covered rice or string-like bodies (especially if the stool wiggles!), apply a herbal worming program immediately. Follow with another dose in two weeks. If you still have not eliminated them, ask a veterinarian. Avoid chemicals whenever possible. They can permanently damage the sensitive lining of the digestive tract of animals, especially younger ones.

Herbal worming can be successful if you follow the directions carefully. Often, the products need to be administered along with fasting for optimum effect. Intestinal worms such as roundworms feed off of old fecal material backed up in the colon. These parasites cannot thrive in a clean, healthy gut. Look for products which contain herbs such as *Rhubarb Root*, which is especially effective against round and threadworms; *Cayenne*, which helps to eliminate eggs; *Barberry Root, Senna Leaves, Wormwood, Quassia Bark* (this works well on Giardia); *Black Walnut Hulls, Neem,* or *Bilva Herb* (excellent general dewormers). *Heartworm*, as well as other blood parasites, can be addressed with this combination. Homeopathic heartworm nosodes are available and have been proven to be good for the elimination and prevention of infestation. *Hawthorn* and *Garlic* are excellent herbs for heart rehabilitation.

Skin Parasites can trigger your pet's allergy-related symptoms, especially chronic skin eruptions or infections. Have your pet carefully examined for skin parasites to find out if they are the source of your pet's symptoms. Avoid the use of medicated or chemical-based topical pest control treatments, which could compromise the immune system and increase your dog's sensitivity to toxins.

Regardless of your findings, the immune system imbalance remains the fundamental issue that needs to be addressed, since pests do not generally invade non-toxic dogs. Waste products being exuded through the skin invite and feed fleas and ticks. Yeast, commonly used to ward off these pests, may become toxic to the liver, increasing instances of infestation. Yeast also promotes ear wax and debris, which will provide a birthing area for bacterial and yeast infections, which in turn can attract ear mites.

Parasitic Infestations Associated with Skin Conditions

Mites are vicious skin parasites that burrow down into the epidermis, causing *Mange*, which prompts a great deal of discomfort and irritation. Scratching and chewing can quickly lead to an infection with discharge. Puppies and chronically ill or elderly pets are particularly susceptible to Demodactic Mange, especially those who have recently been vaccinated. Puppies are most often infested first by the bitch (who may not be symptomatic herself with mange, but may have mites) and become symptomatic themselves after their young immune systems are compromised.

Although pups may grow out of mange by their first birthday as their immune system matures, they can be very debilitated by chronic mange. It can be widespread on the body, but often stays localized on the head and neck, where it causes skin inflammation and spreading patterns of rashes and hair loss. Treat it topically with a daily solution of twelve drops of *Grapefruit Extract*, six drops each of *Tea Tree Oil*, *Golden Seal Root Extract*, and *Pau d'Arco Extract*, two drops of *Yucca Extract*, and three tablespoons freshly squeezed *lemon juice* diluted in two ounces of *Witch Hazel* and four ounces of distilled water. Let the pup air dry and leave the affected area uncovered.

Ear Mites or Otodectes are tiny, white, spider-like pests, that are practically impossible to see with the naked eye. They leave debris resembling finely ground pepper, resulting in a gritty discharge. To dissolve a suspected infestation, follow my recommendations for the removal of an object from the ear. Allow the ear oil to set for at least one-half hour to suffocate the mites. Finish by massaging the base of the ear to loosen the debris further before flushing the ear with a cleaning solution. Repeat several times per day until all the mites are removed, usually within a day or two.

Fleas and Ticks can create a lot of problems for the skin, and if the infestation is allowed to continue, it will make treating skin conditions impossible. These pests are not only weakening your pet, they can infect him with a more serious disease. *Diatomaceous Earth* is tiny, ground-up fossils which dehydrate the pest's outer coating, killing it. Use only food-grade powder. This earth can provide an effective barrier between your home or yard and the pests. Clean your pet and her bedding well with a natural insecticide shampoo and follow with a natural dip. Follow the directions carefully. Groom your pet every day to help remove pests, along with dead skin. This will make skin treatments easier.

Ringworm is a fungal infection which can prompt many symptoms associated with allergies: skin inflammation, itching, and hot spots. Ringworm is evidenced by a small, circular area bare of hair and very irritated. Your pet may scratch at it, causing a bacterial infection. Treat it topically with mange solution or apply some lavender oil.

Seek additional herbal or homeopathic support, according to the symptoms, when needed. *Red Clover Blossoms, Stinging Nettle Leaf, Cleavers Herb, Yellow Dock Root, Burdock Root, Yarrow Flowers, Plantain Leaf and Corm, Licorice Root,* and *Prickly Ash Bark* are excellent herbs to use for skin disorders such as mange. *Spilanthes Leaf and Root, Grape Root, Juniper Berry, Usnea Lichen,* and *Myrrh Gum* can be used together to reverse ringworm, as can *Sarsaparilla* (both can be used topically and internally). Homeopathic *Tellurium* is a primary ringworm remedy, especially when the eczema is localized behind the ears and neck. In a pinch, *Arsenicum* works as well on most skin parasite-related cases.

How to Be Your Vet's Best Friend

The most important ally that you can have, in taking care of your pet, is a trusted veterinarian. You should never think that you can handle each and every health concern on your own. You can however, manage your pet's health care yourself, while making all medically-related decisions using the expertise and guidance of a competent professional. Rely on your veterinarian to explain specific genetic weaknesses and local health concerns so that you can develop a sound preventative program around your pet's individual needs.

Yearly health exams and occasional blood work can help catch an imbalance early, before it becomes a health problem. Often an imbalance in the endocrine system, protein assimilation, or blood sugar irregularities can be spotted long before the actual symptoms, such as allergies or organ failure, show themselves. This can make the difference between simply reversing an acute weakness or having a chronic condition develop. Proper diagnosis to verify a specific imbalance can make the difference between addressing the problem head-on and more successfully, or trying a "hit or miss" therapy that can go on for months. Monitoring the body as it responds to the chosen therapy will also help you identify generally what is, or isn't, working.

Today, there are more holistically-oriented veterinarians who are well versed in the complementary modalities of nutritional therapy, herbs, homeopathy, acupuncture, massage and chiropractic care. Some have even expanded to incorporate esoteric therapies of sound, light and energy healing. In addition, a large number of allopathic (traditionally trained) veterinarians now realize that natural pet care has its place within their traditional, medically-based treatments.

Unfortunately, many of us have had very negative experiences with veterinarians—especially those allopathically trained veterinarians who are unfamiliar with natural care and thus are uncompromising. We may now avoid seeking veterinary support. Possibly, they have spoken to us as if we did not have a clue in our heads about our pet's health care needs, or dismissed our attempts to seek a chemical-free lifestyle for our pets. More likely, they simply failed to address past conditions successfully, and we have lost faith in the medical approach. I am hoping that by giving you a little insight as to what can be successfully accomplished with natural modalities, while encouraging you to join forces with your veterinarian—rather than give them unchallenged authority over your pet's medical care—will help empower you so that you can successfully incorporate proper veterinary care in your pet's holistic lifestyle.

It is vital that you seek a veterinarian who is willing to listen to you, is thorough in their examination and diagnosis, will explain what it is that they recommend and why—but most importantly—will treat you and your pet with respect. If you do not like the way a veterinarian approaches your pet or speaks to you, then find another no matter who recommended them.

It becomes very frustrating for a diagnostician when a pet owner doesn't have the most basic information, and puts the veterinarian (who cares) at a disadvantage—in properly identifying what might be a the bottom of the pet's symptoms. Soon, such veterinarians become jaded and assume that all their clients simply don't have a clue. Who can blame them? Open the lines of communication. Learn more about the choices you make and the recommendations given to you by all concerned parties. You know your pet best and this information will help your companion receive better veterinary care.

By making the necessary changes in their lifestyle and health care before a serious problem or chronic condition develops, you will keep them healthy. Prevention is the best cure!

THE CROSSING PRESS POCKET PET SERIES

Allergies
By Lisa Newman
$6.95 • Paper
ISBN 1-58091-002-5

Arthritis
By Lisa Newman
$6.95 • Paper
ISBN 1-58091-003-3

Natural Cat
By Lisa Newman
$6.95 • Paper
ISBN 1-58091-001-7

Nutrition
By Lisa Newman
$6.95 • Paper
ISBN 1-58091-004-1

Parasites
By Lisa Newman
$6.95 • Paper
ISBN 1-58091-006-8

Skin & Coat Care
By Lisa Newman
$6.95 • Paper
ISBN 1-58091-008-4

Training without Trauma
By Lisa Newman
$6.95 • Paper
ISBN 1-58091-007-6

To receive a current catalog from The Crossing Press
please call toll-free, 800-777-1048.
www.crossingpress.com